OCCUPIED TERRITORIES OF BHARAT

OCCUPIED TERRITORIES OF BHARAT

Alok Bansal & Nidhi Bahuguna

JAMMU KASHMIR STUDY CENTRE

Occupied Territories of Bharat
by Alok Bansal & Nidhi Bahuguna

First Published in 2020

Copyright © Alok Bansal

All rights reserved. No part of this publication may be reproduced, stored in a retrieval system, or transmitted, in any form or by any means, electronic, mechanical, photocopying, recording, or otherwise, without first obtaining written permission of the copyright owner.

Disclaimer: The views and opinions expressed in the book are the individual assertion of the Authors.

Published by
PENTAGON PRESS LLP
206, Peacock Lane, Shahpur Jat,
New Delhi-110049
Phones: 011-64706243, 26491568
Telefax: 011-26490600
website: www.pentagonpress.in

Printed at Aegean Offset Printers, Greater Noida, U.P.

Contents

	Preface	ix
1	**Introduction**	1
	Minor Disputes	3
	Major Disputes	5
	Conclusion	8
2	**Ladakh and J&K:** **Historical Background**	11
	Early History	12
	Consolidation of Jammu and Kashmir under the Dogras	15
	Gilgit Agency	17
3	**Developments in 1947-1949**	25
	Tribal invasion of Jammu and Kashmir	28
	Events leading to the occupation of Gilgit-Baltistan	31
	Occupation of Baltistan	36
	The Siege of Skardu	37
	UN Resolutions	39
	Present Legal Position	40
	The Karachi Agreement, April 28, 1949	41
4	**Pakistan Occupied Jammu and Kashmir (POJK)**	46
	Geography and Administrative Divisions	47
	Socio-political Evolution	50
	Myth of Autonomy	54

v

	People, Culture and Languages of Mirpur-Muzzafarabad (POJK)	58
	Parties and Politics in 'AJK'	62
	Pakistani Army and its Terror Camps	63
	Politics of Water	66
	Human Right Abuses	67
	Economics of Control	69
	Civil Society in POJK	70
5	**Pakistan Occupied Territory of Ladakh (POTL)**	**77**
	The Land and the People	79
	The Economic Potential	83
	Northern Areas	88
	Discontentment with Pakistan	89
	Strategic Importance of Gilgit-Baltistan for India	93
	Security Concerns for India	94
	Water Concerns for India	95
6	**Chinese Occupied Territory of Ladakh (COTL)**	**100**
	Aksai Chin	**104**
	Geography and History	104
	Understanding the Aksai Chin Dispute	106
	Johnson Line	110
	Johnson-Ardagh Line	111
	Macartney-MacDonald Line	111
	Indian Independence and Chinese Occupation	112
	Present Status	115
	Trans-Karakoram Tracts	**116**
	Shaksgam Valley	**118**
	Present State of Shaksgam	121
	Raskam Valley	**122**
	Claims of Hunza in Raskam	124
	Taghdumbash Pamir	**126**
	Minsar	**129**
	Present Position of Minsar	131
7	**Shrines in Occupied Territories**	**136**
	Shrines, Temples and Gurudwaras in POJK	136
	Sharda Temple and University	137
	Current Status	143
	Other Temples and Shrines	144

CONTENTS

Shrines in Gilgit Baltistan (POTL)		145
Kargah Buddha		146
Manthal Buddha Rock		146
Other Buddhist Shrines		149
Gurudwara in Skardu		150
8	**Conclusion**	**153**

APPENDICES

A	UNCIP Resolution of August 13, 1948	163
B	Karachi Agreement	167
C	Sino-Pak Boundary Agreement	173
D	Peace Treaty Between Ladakh and Tibet at Tingmosgang (1684)	179
E	Treaty of Chushul	182

Preface

Every Bhartiya is familiar with the map of Bharat, but very few are aware of the fact that it is the de jure map of Bharat. The de facto map of Bharat, which shows parts of Bhartiya territory under foreign occupation, is something which is amazingly not a part of national debates. The areas between the de jure map and the de facto map carry millions of untold stories, history, cultural linkages with Bharat and the extremely traumatic story of their occupation. The setback in 1962 Sino-Indian War has shaped the national psyche, but surprisingly, the story of the land occupied in the war remains untold. Kailash Mansarovar Yatra is a lasting symbol of Bhartiya tradition, but the story of Minsar, which maintained Kailash Mansarovar has been relegated to some obscure corner of Bhartiya consciousness. Discussions about 1965 war never connect it to Pakistan's unfinished agenda of occupying Jammu and Kashmir. Battle for Siachen and Kargil conflict are discussed without mentioning the fact these could only be launched due to Pakistan's occupation of Bhartiya territory in Ladakh.

Ladakh and Jammu & Kashmir are often called strategically the most significant part of Bharat, but the real strategic areas are those under foreign occupation. Gilgit-Baltistan is an example of multifaceted pluralism, it is an area endowed with rich history, diverse cultures, ethnicities and languages, but for decades the area has been out of Bhartiya consciousness. The citizens of Bharat, living in occupied territories have been facing immense hardships and their human rights have been trampled with impunity, without generating any outrage, both within the country as well as internationally.

With the abrogation of Article 35A and partial abrogation of Article 370, a significant step was taken towards national integration. However, the next logical step towards integration entails getting territories under foreign occupation back under Bhartiya fold. The book is an attempt to lift the veil of darkness that has engulfed the occupied territories and to highlight their different facets, so that the reader gets an insight and understanding of these significant but forgotten lands.

1
Introduction

All Indians have grown up drawing map of India, with which they are extremely familiar; however, a large majority of them are not aware that there are significant areas of Indian territory that are not currently under the effective administrative control of Indian Government. We are familiar with the 'de jure' map of India, but the 'de facto' map of India, showing dotted lines, deals with areas not under the control of India. Even amongst those who are aware of the de facto map, there is little or no knowledge about these areas that have been under the adverse possession of other countries. Historically, the Himalayas were perceived as an impregnable wall that could not be breached. Unfortunately, this myth was rudely shattered, when large swathes of Indian Territory were occupied by Pakistan and China in quick succession after Indian independence.

Indian territorial claims are based on international treaties that were historically signed between British India and other countries, as well as the perceived extent of the territorial limits of the former princely states. India shares its land borders with Afghanistan, Pakistan, China, Nepal, Bhutan, Myanmar and Bangladesh. It shares its maritime boundaries with Pakistan, Maldives, Sri Lanka, Bangladesh, Myanmar, Thailand and Indonesia. Of all these countries, India has no dispute with Afghanistan, Maldives and Bhutan.[1] With Indonesia and Thailand, boundaries are clearly delineated.

India through protracted negotiations has managed to resolve some outstanding disputes with Sri Lanka and Bangladesh. With Sri Lanka, contentious issue of maritime boundary was resolved and claims over Kachchativu Island were given up. More significantly, contentious boundary disputes with Bangladesh have been resolved. The historical problem of enclaves within each other's territory has been resolved by transferring them en masse. Here again, India showed magnanimity and maturity in not insisting on rigid equality of territory transferred. India even agreed to relocate 979 Indian citizens, who did not wish to remain in Bangladesh. During Prime Minister Modi's visit to Bangladesh in June 2015, the Land Boundary Agreement between India and Bangladesh of 1974 and its Protocol of 2011 were ratified.[2] Similarly, there were lands in adverse possession (areas contiguous to the border, legally part of one country, but occupied by citizens of other country), which were also resolved. Undemarcated borders

INTRODUCTION

between India and Bangladesh of approximately 6.1 km in three sectors, Daikhata-56 (West Bengal), Muhuri River-Belonia (Tripura) and Lathitila-Dumabari (Assam) were also resolved.[3] Consequently, with the implementation of the Land Boundary Agreement and Protocol of 2011, all outstanding land boundary issues between India and Bangladesh have been resolved.[4]

Even more contentious was the maritime boundary between the two countries, as the concave coastline ensured that Bangladesh maritime zones were sandwiched landwards by Indian and Myanmar's maritime zones. The problem was further accentuated by the emergence of New Moore Island near the mouth of Haribhanga River, which was claimed by both the countries. However, the submergence of the island due to rising sea levels removed this irritant.[5] Subsequently, the two countries approached an arbitration tribunal for delimitation of maritime boundary. The tribunal gave its award on 7 July 2014 and settled the maritime boundary between India and Bangladesh.[6] Even though the award was seen to be against India and there were strong legal grounds for appeal, in the spirit of mutual bonhomie, India decided not to appeal.

Minor Disputes

There is no border dispute between India and Myanmar. However, certain sectors of India-Myanmar boundary remain to be demarcated, which pertains to the alignment of nine boundary pillars (BPs) with Myanmar in Manipur. This creates minor perceptional differences, which lead to media reports about protests against fencing work in Manipur at the India-Myanmar border on grounds that the fence was being constructed deep inside Indian Territory. Replying to a question in Rajya Sabha, Kiren Rijiju, the then Minister of State for Home had categorically denied destruction of any border pillars and had affirmed that the demarcation of nine BPs was being worked in an atmosphere of complete understanding with Myanmar. He stated that out of 1472-km-long boundary between the two countries, 171 km was to be demarcated through a mutually agreed demarcation mechanism.[7]

India and Myanmar have been having a regular dialogue on unresolved issues related to boundary demarcation and border management. These dialogues take place through institutionalised mechanisms, such as Foreign Office Consultations, National Level Meetings (NLM) and Sectoral Level Meetings (SLM). Meetings are also held at the level of the Heads of Survey Department and Director (Survey), where issues related to boundary demarcation, joint survey, inspection and maintenance of BPs are, inter alia, discussed. Joint survey, inspection and maintenance of BPs are regularly carried out by Survey Departments of both the sides. India has also proposed constitution of a Joint Boundary Working Group with Myanmar to enable examination of all boundary-related issues in a comprehensive manner.

Similarly, with Nepal there are some minor differences of perception over boundary alignment. Although strip maps covering almost 98 per cent of India–Nepal border

INTRODUCTION

have been jointly finalised and ratified by both the countries, there are differing opinions on the alignment of border territories in some areas like Kalapani in Uttarakhand and Narsahi-Susta in Bihar. The two sides have set up a high-level bilateral mechanism to discuss the matter, with technical inputs from the India-Nepal Boundary Working Group.[8]

The dispute involves Kalapani with an area of 400 square kilometres and Susta with an area of 140 square kilometres. Kalapani, which is at the trijunction of India, China and Nepal, has strategic relevance and has been with India since independence. There are differences as to where Mahakali River, which defines border between India and Nepal, originates. This would determine as to where does Lipulekh Pass lie. Although the 1954 trade agreement between India and China mentioned it as one of the passes that could be used for Indo-Tibetan trade and pilgrimage to Kailash Mansarovar, Nepal claims it to be in its territory. Similarly, Susta in Bihar is claimed by Nepal as a part of its Lumbini district. The Narayani River (known as Gandak in India) marks the Indian-Nepali border. However, over the years, several large floods have resulted in the river changing its course. This has resulted in a dispute over 14,500 hectares of land. A technical group comprising officials from the two countries has been discussing the issues since 1998, but it has not yet been resolved.

Major Disputes

Most serious differences over territory and boundary exist

with China and Pakistan. With regards to Pakistan, it claims entire union territories of Jammu and Kashmir as well as Ladakh as its part. It stakes claims on the entire princely state of Jammu and Kashmir as it existed in 1947. Not only that, in the turbulence that followed the independence in 1947, it annexed large chunks of territory in the former princely state of Jammu and Kashmir, before the Maharaja could even accede to India. It therefore has large chunks of territory of both Ladakh and Jammu Kashmir under its illegal occupation. It has also entered into an illegal agreement with China, whereby it has ceded large chunks of territory to China in Ladakh.

Outside Jammu and Kashmir, the only dispute between India and Pakistan pertains to Sir Creek, which is a 96-km strip of water in the marshlands between India and Pakistan called Rann of Kutch. Pakistan claims the line to follow the eastern shore of the estuary while India claims a center line (differing interpretations of paragraphs 9 and 10 of the Bombay Government Resolution of 1914 signed between then the Government of Sindh and Rao Maharaj of Kutch). This has affected the maritime boundary delineation in the waters of Arabian Sea between the two countries. Before India's independence, the provincial region was a part of the Bombay Presidency of British India. After India's independence in 1947, Sindh became a part of Pakistan while Kutch remained a part of India, Indian Army and Pak Marines are deployed on both sides of the border.

With China, India has a huge boundary dispute almost

INTRODUCTION

all along its boundary. China claims a large territory in Ladakh and has occupied a significant chunk of this territory in 1962. In addition, Pakistan has gifted it a large chunk of land as part of the 1963 Sino-Pak Agreement. There are also other significant parts of the territory of former princely state of Jammu and Kashmir, which are under Chinese control, including some that have not even been claimed by India as its territory. However, unlike Pakistan, China claims territories in other parts of India as well. It claims most of Arunachal Pradesh, some parts in Himachal Pradesh and Uttarakhand and some passes in Sikkim. China does not recognise McMahon Line, boundary between Tibet and India for the eastern sector, drawn by British negotiator Henry McMahon and signed by British and Tibetan representatives, in Simla in March 1914.

This dispute led to the 1962 War between the two countries. Barring small pieces of land in the Central Sector (Himachal Pradesh and Uttarakhand) and some passes in Sikkim, the major dispute between the two countries remains in Ladakh and Arunachal Pradesh, where dispute pertains to thousands of square kilometres of land. However, although it does not recognise McMahon Line, barring small pieces, it does not physically occupy significant land in Arunachal Pradesh. On the other hand, it has occupied large tracts of land in Ladakh, both before and after the 1962 War with India. Its possession in Ladakh has been further augmented on account of transfer of Shaksgam Valley by Pakistan after the signing of Sino-Pak Agreement of 1963. The two countries have been making efforts to resolve this dispute and have a Special Representative (SR) each to explore the framework for a boundary settlement from the political perspective of the overall bilateral relationship. There have been 21 meetings of SRs, with the last meeting being held in Chengdu on 24 November 2018. The two sides have agreed to seek a fair, reasonable and mutually acceptable solution to the boundary question through dialogue and peaceful negotiations.

Conclusion

As a result, it is clear that barring some small pieces of land in Arunachal Pradesh, Sikkim, Uttarakhand and Himachal Pradesh, most of the Indian territory that is under the control of foreign occupation lies within the Union Territories of Ladakh and Jammu and Kashmir and was an integral part of the princely state of Jammu and Kashmir that was ruled by Maharaja Hari Singh in 1947. This book would primarily deal with these territories of J&K and Ladakh that are under the occupation of Pakistan and China.

Although both the territories are constitutionally an integral part of India and under foreign occupation, the two cases differ significantly. The region under Chinese occupation, which includes the trans-Karakoram Shaksgam Valley, unilaterally ceded by Pakistan to it in 1963 as part of a boundary settlement, Principality of Minsar and Aksai Chin and Western Ladakh, militarily occupied by China in 1962, is by and large devoid of major habitation, and as

INTRODUCTION

such needs to be dealt with separately. It would be infructuous to analyse its administration and the treatment of its people as there are virtually none. Moreover, China does not claim Jammu and Kashmir but only a part of Ladakh and its dispute with India is a border dispute and not a territorial one. On the other hand, both India and Pakistan claim the former princely state of Jammu and Kashmir in its entirety as their integral part, although Pakistan has bequeathed a part under its occupation to China in 1963.

More significantly, since the Simla Accord of 1972, the Line of Control (LoC) between India and Pakistan from International Border to Point NJ 9842 has been clearly delineated on map and demarcated on ground. On the other hand, Line of Actual Control (LAC) between Indian and Chinese positions in Ladakh has neither been delineated on map, nor demarcated on ground. The book will attempt to look at these regions historically and try and throw some light on their historical evolution, current geography and where applicable, the population.

NOTES

1. As stated by Shri V Muraleedharan, the Minister of State in the Ministry of External Affairs in reply to unstarred question number 881 on 26 June 2019 in Lok Sabha, from https://www.mea.gov.in/lok-sabha.htm?dtl/31485/question+no881+indopak+ border+ dispute (accessed on 10 December 2019)
2. Ibid.
3. Shubhajit Roy, "Everything you need to know: Land swap in offing with Bangladesh to end disputes", *The Indian Express*, December 2, 2014.

4   As stated by Shri V Muraleedharan, op. cit.
5   "Island India, Bangla fought over drowns", *The Telegraph*, March 25, 2010.
6   Naomi Burke, "Annex VII Arbitral Tribunal Delimits Maritime Boundary Between Bangladesh and India in the Bay of Bengal", *American Society of International Law*, Volume 18, Issue 20, dated September 22, 2014.
7   "No border dispute between India and Myanmar states government", *The Economic Times*, August 02, 2018. From https://economictimes.indiatimes.com/news/defence/no-border-dispute-between-india-and-myanmar-states-government/articleshow/65229882.cms?from=mdr (10 December 2019)
8   As stated by Shri V Muraleedharan, op. cit.

2

Ladakh and J&K: Historical Background

Both Ladakh and Jammu Kashmir, have been part of India's political and cultural domain and spiritual consciousness off and on for over 3000 years dating back to Mahabharata. These linkages are manifestly visible in Ganpatyar and Khir Bhavani temples in the Valley, as well as Shankaracharya temple, which is perched on top of a hill that dominates Srinagar. In third century BC, Emperor Ashoka introduced Buddhism in Kashmir and subsequently, Emperor Kanishka held the Fourth Buddhist Council in the valley, where 500 Buddhist monks from across the world participated. Emperor Lalitaditya's reign from 724 to 760 A.D., marked the golden age of Kashmir. Islam came in gradually in the 14th century giving birth to a vibrant, syncretic sufi-rishi tradition of Kashmiriyat that has since been undermined by today's jihadis.[1]

There is widespread ignorance about the historical background of Ladakh and Jammu & Kashmir, which has perpetuated various myths about the evolution of the princely state of 'Jammu and Kashmir'. Some of these include the belief that the princely state of Jammu and Kashmir, which was the predecessor of the two union territories of Ladakh and J&K, was an artificial entity created by the Dogras. There is a mistaken belief that the entire region was never a part of the same political dispensation. Another myth being perpetuated by Pakistan is about Gilgit-Baltistan, the territory of Ladakh under Pakistan's illegal occupation. Pakistan has been attempting to showcases the existence of this region as a separate political entity, distinct from Ladakh and the former princely State of Jammu and Kashmir. There is another belief that it was an indigenous movement by the local population that actually led to the separation of Gilgit-Baltistan from the State of Jammu and Kashmir. All these are nothing but attempts to merge Gilgit-Baltistan with Pakistan and recent campaign to make it the fifth province of Pakistan, so that international apprehensions on China Pakistan Economic Corridor (CPEC), could be assuaged.

Early History

It is now an established fact that all parts of Jammu and Kashmir were included in the wide dominions of the great Kushan Dynasty. It is adequately proved by the combined evidence of Buddhist records and the coins, copper pieces of Kanishka and Huvishka that are found in abundance at many of the old sites of Jammu and Kashmir. According to

Buddhist tradition, Kanishka, who ruled from 78 AD to 140 AD, held the fourth Buddhist council in Kashmir and Huen Tsiang on his visit to the Valley found that the memory of the ruler was fully alive in the kingdom. In fact, the Mahayana or the Northern school of Buddhism originated in Kashmir and attained pre-eminence during Kanishka's Buddhist council.[2]

Buddhism suffered a setback in Kashmir after the reign of Kanishka and his immediate successors. During the subsequent Hindu Period, under Lalitaditya (724-761 AD) and the Karkota kings who followed, almost all the regions of the Jammu and Kashmir State as it existed under the Dogra empire were integral parts of the Kashmir Empire. Not only that, Lalitaditya's empire extended all the way from central Asia, Afghanistan down to South India thereby indicating Kashmir's close historical ties with the rest of India. However, whenever the leadership in Kashmir was weak, the peripheral regions attained independence.[3]

Thereafter, even during the Muslim period, close relations were maintained by the rulers in Kashmir with Dardistan, Baltistan, Ladakh and Jammu and all other peripheral regions of the state. In fact Rinchin, (1320-1323) the first Muslim king of Kashmir, was a prince of Ladakh. Sultan Shihab-ud-din, who is said to be 'the Lalitaditya of medieval Kashmir', ruled not only over all parts of present day Jammu and Kashmir but extended his empire all the way to the banks of the Sutlej. Throughout the period of the Sultanate there was constant interaction amongst the people of various parts of Kashmir. Whenever the central authority was strong the peripheral regions accepted its suzerainty but whenever the central authority was weak, they would declare their independence. In fact, the interaction of Kashmir with Dardistan, Baltistan, Ladakh and Jammu continued unabated during this period and the rulers of the last major independent Muslim dynasty that ruled Kashmir – The Chak dynasty – had migrated from Gilgit.[4]

With the ascension of Mughals, Kashmir became a province of the Delhi empire in 1540 AD and continued to be ruled by its governors for the next three centuries. During this period, Mughal emperors visited Kashmir on a number of occasions and built many monuments. This period saw an increase in the interaction between Kashmir and the rest of India. Close political, cultural, social and economic links were established between Kashmir and other parts of India. With the weakening of Mughal empire Kashmir came to be ruled by Afghan kings for around six decades. Thereafter, with the rise of Sikh power in Punjab, Kashmir became a part of the Sikh empire in 1819 AD.[5] By this time the peripheral regions of the state had become independent of the central authority in Srinagar and thus the Sikh rule was initially confined to the Kashmir Valley whereas the Jammu region was given to Raja Gulab Singh as a *jagir* by Maharaja Ranjit Singh in 1820. After consolidating his position in the Jammu region, Gulab Singh captured Ladakh in 1836 and Baltistan in 1840.[6] On the other hand Gilgit was captured in 1842 by Col Nathu Shah, Commander of Sheikh Ghulam Mohi-ud-din, the Sikh governor of Kashmir.[7]

Consolidation of Jammu and Kashmir under the Dogras

Meanwhile after the defeat of the Sikh army at Subraon in February 1846, the Treaty of Lahore was signed on March 9, 1846. It forced the Sikhs to cede to the British all territories between the Beas and the Sutlej and to pay Rs 1 crore as war indemnity. Lal Singh, the then Prime Minister of the Sikhs, offered all hill territories of the kingdom including Jammu and Kashmir in lieu of the indemnity. British then offered to make Gulab Singh the independent ruler of Jammu and Kashmir provided he paid the indemnity amount. The amount was reduced to Rs 75 lakh as the British decided to keep the territory between the Ravi and the Beas which included Kangra.[8] Accordingly the Treaty of Amritsar was signed, which formalized the creation of a new state of Jammu and Kashmir, the British government having "transferred and made over for ever in independent possession" to "Raja Mian Gulab Singh and heirs male of his body, the territory" which included Kashmir and Jammu.[9] This treaty made Gulab Singh the absolute ruler of Kashmir; he was called the Maharaja of Kashmir and became a full-fledged sovereign of Jammu, Kashmir and Ladakh, as well as Gilgit, Chilas and Baltistan, the region, which was called Northern Areas of Pakistan, without any authority under the International Law.[10]

After this treaty, Gulab Singh, who was already the ruler of Jammu, Ladakh and Baltistan, moved his forces to take possession of Kashmir Valley but they were defeated by the Sikh troops of Sheikh Imam-ud-din. Gulab Singh was forced to summon British help to establish his authority in the Kashmir Valley and thereby unite Jammu with the Valley. It is pertinent to note that the Kashmiris and the Dogras were no strangers. Kalhan's *Rajatarangini*, which covers the history of Kashmir up till 1148 AD, makes innumerable mentions of close contact between the people and rulers of Jammu and Kashmir Valley. Eventually, there were matrimonial alliances between Kashmiri sultans and the families of Jammu rulers. In 1486, during a popular movement in Kashmir against the domination of the Sayyeds, a contingent of Jammu soldiers under the ruler of Jammu came to help the Kashmiris. During the Mughal Period, the interaction between the two regions increased as the most important trade routes between Kashmir and Delhi passed over the Pir Panjal and the Banihal passes. Moreover, when the Kashmiris were suffering under the tyrannical rule of the Afghans, it was Jammu that offered refuge to the thousands of harassed Kashmiris.[11]

By 1850, Gulab Singh had added Buddhist-majority Ladakh, Muslim-majority Baltistan and Muslim-majority Kashmir Valley to Jammu with its Hindu majority population.[12] After he had occupied Kashmir, Col Nathu Shah, who controlled Gilgit on behalf of the Sikhs, transferred his allegiance to Gulab Singh who thus became master of Gilgit as well.[13] The British encouraged Gulab Singh to spread his political influence in Gilgit-Baltistan so as to establish a safe buffer state between Russia and British India.[14] By 1866, the entire region had come under the control of the Dogras and the rulers of Hunza and Nagar became vassals of Kashmir.

Gilgit Agency

Though the British had accepted Gulab Singh's undisputed control over Kashmir, they interfered in the region's administration on the pretext that the Maharaja was inflicting severe hardships on his subjects. The interference was basically necessitated by the growing Russian influence in Central Asia. The British policies towards Kashmir fluctuated with developments in India and Central Asia. At one stage after the 1857 Mutiny, the British contemplated military occupation of Kashmir. But, alarmed by the Russian expansion in Central Asia in 1860s, they cajoled the Maharaja to bring the States of Chitral and Yasin under his control to prevent Russian influence. Gilgit Agency was established in 1877 with Major John Biddulph as the first political agent. However, the agent was withdrawn in 1881 to be reappointed in 1889 in view of the growing Afghan influence in Chitral as well as Russian military activities in Central Asia.[15]

Consequent to the Russian revolution, the British anxieties over the region increased and the Maharaja was forced to lease the Gilgit Agency to the British for 60 years on March 26, 1935. The agreement gave the Viceroy the right to assume civil and military administration of the Wazarat of Gilgit Province that lay beyond the right bank of the river Indus. The Maharaja was in no position to resist the British pressure.[16] As a result, despite being a part of Maharaja's territory, Gilgit and the surrounding regions of Dardistan, including the vassal states, were administered virtually by the British from 1935 to 1947. Their status and relationship with the Kashmir State prior to the lease of Gilgit Agency to the British in 1935 were as follows:

(a) **The Gilgit Wazarat.** It comprised the Tehsils of Gilgit and Astor and the Niabat of Bunji. It was under the direct control of the Kashmir Darbar. The Officer heading the administration was called Wazir-i-Wazarat.

(b) **Hunza and Nagar.** Hunza and Nagar were referred to as States. After a military operation against the States of Hunza and Nagar in 1891, the Maharaja of Kashmir with the approval and authority of the Governor General, installed Muhammad Nazim Khan as the ruler of Hunza. A *sanad* was issued by the Maharaja to the ruler that the Chiefship of the Hunza State would be hereditary. He was assured protection so long as his family remained loyal to the State of Jammu and Kashmir and to the British Government. An annual tribute of 25 *tilloos* of gold, equal to 16 *tolas* and 5 *mashas*, to paid to the State of Jammu and Kashmir, was fixed. A similar *sanad* was issued to the Mir of Nagar, Jaffa Khan. An annual tribute of 26 *tilloos* of gold equal to 17 *tolas* and 1 *masha* was fixed. Both Hunza and Nagar were also paid annual subsidies of Rs 4,000 each.

(c) **Chitral.** The ruler of the Chitral was called Mehtar who acknowledged the suzerainty of the Maharaja of Kashmir, and through him to the British Government in 1878. Unlike other vassal States, Chitral continued its allegiance to the Maharaja and the British Government until 1947.

The Mehtar of Chitral enjoyed the title of 'His Highness' and the right of getting an 11-gun salute.

(d) **Punial.** The district of Punial came under the hands of the Maharaja in 1860. Raja Isa Bahadur was made the local ruler. The Raja of Punial was known for his loyalty to the Maharaja and to the British Government. The ruler received an annual subsidy of Rs 1,200 which was fixed in 1895. In 1927, it was increased to Rs 1,600 paid by the Government of India. Punial did not pay tribute to the Kashmir *Darbar*.

(e) **Yasin and Kuh-Ghizer.** In 1895, Yasin was bifurcated from the Chitral State and brought under the Governorship of the Gilgit Agency. Mehtarjao Abdur Rehman Khan was appointed as the Governor of Yasin in 1895 by the Political Agent in the name of the Maharaja of Kashmir. In 1905, Kuh-Ghizer was brought under the Governorship of Yasin. Later it was separated into two Governorships. The Governors paid part of their revenue to the Kashmir Darbar. Both the Governors received Rs 1,200 annually from Kashmir Darbar as subsidy.

(f) **Ish Kaman.** Ish Kaman was also separated from Chitral and placed under a Governor - a paid official without any hereditary claims. Mir Ali Mardan Shah was first Governor of Ish Kaman. His terms and conditions were same as those of Kuh-Ghizer and Yasin.

(g) **Chilas.** Chilas was occupied in 1893, and placed

under the charge of Assistant Political Agent, Chilas. Chilas paid an annual tribute of Rs 3,000 to Kashmir. On account of the distance from Srinagar and hardship it had to bear, Chilas was given the concession to pay the tribute to Kashmir *Darbar* every third year.

(h) **Gor.** Gor enjoyed special privileges due to its uninterrupted help to the British. Gor paid tribute to Kashmir, through the *Wazir-i-Wazarat* in Gilgit.

(i) **Darel and Tangir.** Darel and Tangir were small, semi-independent states that had accepted the suzerainty of Kashmir. They had caused much trouble to the Gilgit Agency and were effectively brought under control by the British.[17]

After leasing of Gilgit Agency all areas on the right bank of the Indus were administered directly by the British. A modicum of the Maharaja's authority was maintained by way of flying his flag at the official headquarters of the agency and the appointment of certain state officials in Gilgit. However, the only real authority with the Maharaja was to grant mining licences and leases.[18] It is often forgotten that the region to the left of river Indus in Dardistan and the entire Baltistan remained under the direct control of Maharaja. The announcement of independence in 1947, forced the British to hand the Gilgit Agency back to the Maharaja.

Jammu & Kashmir emerged as a distinct political entity in 1846 with the assumption of sovereignty by the Dogra ruler Gulab Singh. Till then, it had successively been a part of the realms of various Hindu, Buddhist, Muslim and Sikh dynasties—each with its centre of political power in other parts of what we today refer to as South Asia. During the rule of the last of these dynasties—the Sikh—Gulab Singh was conferred a fief over Jammu for his contribution to the conquest of Jammu & Kashmir. He subsequently expanded this realm by conquering Ladakh and Baltistan in the late 1830s. With the onset of the decline of Sikh power at the end of the First Anglo-Sikh War in 1846, Gulab Singh espied an opportunity to make even more substantial gains and concluded an agreement with the British colonial authorities in India. Under this Treaty of Amritsar, signed on 16 March 1846, he acknowledged the supremacy of the British Government and in return acquired sovereignty over the hill country between the rivers Indus and Ravi, including Jammu, Kashmir, Ladakh, Gilgit and Baltistan. While he had a free hand in conducting the internal affairs of this State of Jammu & Kashmir as well as to ensure his dynastic succession, Britain—the paramount power—was exclusively responsible, like in the case of all other princely states, for defence, foreign affairs and communications.[19]

Hari Singh's ascendance to the throne of Jammu & Kashmir in 1925 coincided with the awakening of mass political consciousness throughout India, which was spearheaded by a renewed and invigorated Indian National Congress under the direction of Mahatma Gandhi. This found an echo in Jammu & Kashmir as well, though the popular movement in this princely state was directed more at the rule of the Dogra dynasty. During the course of the

1930s, Sheikh Abdullah, who had returned after completing his education at Lahore and Aligarh, spearheaded this popular movement through the medium of the All Jammu & Kashmir Muslim Conference, which he had founded in October 1932 to represent the State's Muslim population. But slowly, Abdullah became dissatisfied with the sectarian approach to political struggle and started making common cause with the Indian National Congress. In June 1939, he transformed the All Jammu & Kashmir Muslim Conference into the All Jammu & Kashmir National Conference. Only three of the 179 delegates attending the special session of the party to effect the transformation, opposed the move.[20] In 1946, the National Conference formally joined the All-India States Peoples' Congress (AISPC), and Abdullah became its president on the eve of Indian independence.[21] It would be pertinent to note here that the AISPC was the Congress party's vehicle for integrating the States Peoples' movements with its own anti-colonial struggle, and its objective was the attainment of full responsible government by the peoples of the princely states as integral parts of free India.[22]

However, the opponents of Abdullah's move within the party teamed up with others of a similar ideological persuasion to revive the All Jammu & Kashmir Muslim Conference in June 1941. This resulted in a growing political-ideological divide in the state similar to, and in effect a carry-over of the ideological struggle between the Congress and the Muslim League in British India.[23] Abdullah's subsequent gesture in requesting Jinnah to mediate between the two parties proved to be a grave mistake and merely contributed to deepening the divide. Jinnah made an extremely partisan statement that "99 per cent of the Moslems who met me are of the opinion that the Moslem Conference alone is the representative organ of the State Moslems." The extremely biased opinion extremely enraged Abdullah and foreclosed any feasibility of future collaboration of the National Conference with Jinnah and his Muslim League.[24]

This is how the princely state of Jammu and Kashmir was on the eve of British departure from India. The above narrative clearly depicts the evolution of the princely state of Jammu and Kashmir under the Dogra rulers and shows the historical linkages of both Ladakh as well as Jammu and Kashmir with rest of Bharatvarsh. It also shows that the territories currently occupied by foreign powers were an integral part of historical Bharat and its cultural consciousness.

NOTES

1. BG Verghese, "A Jammu and Kashmir Primer: From Myth to Reality", Centre for Policy Research, New Delhi, Occasional Paper No 14, p 4.
2. Prithivi Nath Kaul Bamzai, *A History of Kashmir*, Metropolitan Book Company, New Delhi, 1973, p. 73.
3. Ibid, pp. 117-130.
4. Ibid, pp. 305 -374.
5. For this as well as other early historical accounts I have relied on Prithivi Nath Kaul Bamzai's, *A History of Kashmir*.
6. P Stobdan, "North West Under The Maharaja" in Jasjit Singh (ed), *Pakistan Occupied Kashmir: Under The Jackboot*, Siddhi Books, New Delhi, 1995, pp. 39-40.

7   FM Hassnain, *Gilgit : The Northern Gate of India*, Sterling Publishers Pvt Ltd, New Delhi, 1978, p. 27.
8   Balraj Madhok, A story of Bungling in Kashmir, Young Asia Publications, New Delhi, pp. 5-7.
9   NN Raina, Kashmir Politics and Imperialist Manoeuvres 1846-1980, Patriot Publishers, New Delhi, 1988, p. 3.
10 Hilal Ahmad War, *The Great Disclosures: Secrets Unmasked*, Manas Publications, New Delhi, pp. 38-39.
11 Bamzai, op. cit., pp. 654-655.
12 Owen Bennett Jones, "Pakistan Eye of the Storm", Penguin Books India (P) Ltd, New Delhi, 2002, p. 57.
13 Balraj Madhok, op. cit., p. 7.
14 FM Hassnain, op. cit., pp. 27-28.
15 P Stobdan, op. cit., p. 22.
16 Ibid, pp. 31-36.
17 Ibid pp. 36 -38.
18 Amar Singh Chohan, "The Gilgit Agency 1877-1935", Atlantic Publishers and Distributors, New Delhi, p. 220.
19 V.P. Menon, *Integration of the Indian States* (Orient Longman: Chennai, 1961 paperback edn, 1997 reprint), pp. 390-91; Josef Korbel, *Danger in Kashmir* (Princeton University Press: Princeton, N.J., 1966 2nd edn.), pp. 12-14.
20 Prem Nath Bazaz, *Kashmir in Crucible* (Pamposh Publications: New Delhi, 1967), pp. 34-35.
21 C. Dasgupta, *War and Diplomacy in Kashmir 1947-48* (Sage Publications: New Delhi, 2002), p. 35.
22 Sisir Gupta, *Kashmir: A Study in India-Pakistan Relations* (Asia Publishers: Bombay, 1966), p. 37.
23 Matin Zuberi, "The Problem of Kashmir," in Guy Wint, ed., *Asia Handbook* (Penguin Books: Harmondsworth, Middlesex, 1969 edn.), p. 505.
24 Cited in Lord Birdwood, *Two Nations and Kashmir* (Gulshan Books: Srinagar, 2005 reprint), p. 62.

3

Developments in 1947-1949

In 1947, when Maharaja Hari Singh, the ruler of princely state of Jammu and Kashmir was deciding which of the two dominions he should accede to, Pakistan virtually forced his hand by unleashing tribal militia led by Pakistani army officers to invade the State. From the moment of its birth, Pakistan had made Kashmir a central pillar of its policy. As far as the Muslim League was concerned, the fact that Pakistan's "very name ... included Kashmir" clearly indicated that its leadership could never have considered an independent Kashmir. Jinnah often told his followers that Kashmir "will fall into our lap like a ripe fruit". He was totally convinced "that a dispassionate consideration of the relevant facts of population and geography, the economic and cultural ties, and even the Maharaja's dynastic interest would inevitably point toward accession with Pakistan".[1]

The Dilemma of Maharaja Hari Singh was that his state had borders with both Pakistan and India as well as with Afghanistan, China and the Soviet Union. He was a Hindu ruler, who ruled over a population that then comprised a little over 77 per cent Muslims. His army constituted over one third Muslims and his administration was a mix of Muslims, Hindus and Sikhs. Staying Independent was not an option. There was a 'Maharaja Quit Kashmir' movement against the Maharaja since 1946 led by Sheikh Abdullah. Acceding to India was an attractive option given its secular credentials and cultural connect. However, Maharaja felt that this would result in the political empowerment of Abdullah and his own loss of power, status and prestige, as the Congress party and especially Nehru were extremely supportive of Sheikh Abdullah, who was then serving a jail sentence for launching the 'Quit Kashmir' movement against the Maharaja in 1946. Sardar Patel, however, wrote to the Maharaja and tried to alleviate his apprehensions.[2]

On the other hand, acceding to Pakistan prima facie, appeared to be a better option, as the Muslim League under Jinnah had repeatedly assured him complete internal sovereignty. The Maharaja had also received pledges of continued loyalty, though conditional upon his opting for Pakistan, from the leaders of the Muslim Conference and, telegraphically, from the chieftains of Chitral, Hunza and other small outlying territories of the state. But some of these pledges soon turned into threats of military invasion, as happened in the case of the Mehtar of Chitral and the Nawab of Dir. Maharaja rightly realised that, given the extreme emotions evoked by communal polarisation, his accession to Pakistan would eventually lead to him being divested of his rule over the Muslim-majority population. Added to this were events like the Direct action day of 1946 unfolding, followed by migration of thousands of Hindu and Sikh families from Pakistan carrying horror stories. He clearly appreciated that any communal disturbance could bring his government to a grinding halt and ultimately make his position and rule totally defenceless and untenable.[3]

In an attempt to temporarily maintain the *status quo*, he sought 'Standstill Agreements' with both Dominions, for which he sent identical telegrams to the two governments on 12 August 1947. Pakistan telegraphically conveyed its consent to this arrangement on 15 August, which provided for the continuation of administrative arrangements for communications, supplies, posts and telegraphs. India, for its part, telegraphed back an invitation for the Maharaja or one of his duly authorised ministers to fly to Delhi for the purpose of negotiating a standstill agreement.[4] The Government of India's stated policy, which was announced on 01 August 1947 was, "no standstill agreement without accession". It had been framed to specifically counter the clamour for 'no to accession' amongst the princely states.[5] Although no standstill agreement was signed between India and Jammu and Kashmir, the existing arrangements between the two remained in practice.

The Indian Government was aware since July 1947

about preparations afoot in Pakistan's Punjab and North West Frontier Province to invade Jammu and Kashmir. The correspondence between Home Minister Patel, Prime Minister Nehru and Maharaja Hari Singh proved that by end of September 1947, the Indian Government was very much aware of Pakistan's plans to send raiders into Jammu and Kashmir. They were also aware of Pakistan's hand in fuelling dissent in Poonch. The advice of the Government of India to Maharaja was to release Sheikh Abdullah and make him the prime minister of Jammu and Kashmir to gather mass support against Pakistani invasions and then accede to India.[6] All this while, when India was aiding Maharaja Hari Singh to come to a decision, and Jinnah was expressing his wish to visit Jammu and Kashmir in mid-September; Pakistan was planning to militarily overthrow the Maharaja's government and engineer the State's accession to Pakistan, by fermenting discontent and supporting a rebellion in Poonch.[7]

Tribal invasion of Jammu and Kashmir

According to Maj. Gen. Scott, the commander of the State Forces, towards the end of August 1947, around 30 Pakistani nationals infiltrated into Poonch and began inciting the Sutti and Sudhan tribes there to start protests against Maharaja, in support of accession to Pakistan. Consequently, in early September, a march was undertaken by around 10,000 local residents to Poonch to air their local grievances. The protests were mainly regarding high food prices, although some pro-Pakistan slogans were also raised. On 9 September 1947, the State troops dispersed them at the town of Bagh, resulting in death of 20 demonstrators. Sardar Abdul Qayyum Khan, who was the principal organiser of the demonstration, along with three of his accomplices fled to the mountains and started organising armed resistance against the forces of the State. According to Scott, there was no further trouble till the end of his tenure on 29 September 1947. [8] Poonch had 60,000 demobilised soldiers who were the mainstay of the uprising.[9]

To further increase the pressure on Maharaja, Pakistan violated the standstill agreement and stopped supplying essential food items and fuel to Kashmir. The excuse given by Pakistan authorities was that Muslims drivers were being killed by Hindus and Sikhs, which was a blatant lie and has been clearly denied by Scott.[10] All this while the clashes and raids were going in areas of Jammu and Poonch, where the local Muslim population at places had turned against the state forces and was helping the raiders in targeting Hindus and Sikhs. The larger part of Maharaja's forces at this point was deployed in Poonch, Bhimber, Mirpur, Mangala and Kotli area.[11]

The authorities in Pakistan had entrusted the operations North of Rawalpindi along Jammu and Kashmir's border with North West Frontier Province (NWFP) to Khurshid Anwar, a former British Indian Army officer. He mobilised tribals from NWFP, who had already been radicalised to launch a *jihad* and owned large number of motorised vehicles, thereby solving the logistical problem of carrying the raiders across. The Muslim officers and men of the 4th

Battalion of Maharaja's army, who were guarding the bridges on the border, were co-opted in the plan. The Muslim troops killed their non-Muslim colleagues, while sleeping, and ensured that there were no forces guarding the bridges to stop the raiders, when the invasion started on the night of 21/22 October 1947. Muzaffarabad, Uri and Baramulla were attacked, raiders indulging in looting, raping and killing Hindus and Sikhs. At Baramulla, they stayed on for looting thus delaying the attack on Srinagar.[12]

The forces of the Maharaja were hopelessly outnumbered but they valiantly defended their posts. Brigadier Rajendra Singh fought to the last man and was awarded the first Mahavir Chakra of independent India. Muslims who helped Hindus were also killed. It is pertinent to note that under Maharaja's rule, all Muslim troops in the State force were from either from Jammu region (mainly Poonch) or from Mirpur-Muzaffarabad belt. There were also some troops and officers from Gilgit-Baltistan but none from Kashmir Valley as Kashmiris were not considered a martial race. The Maharaja approached the Indian Government for help and acceded to the dominion of India on 26 October 1947. Indian forces landed in Srinagar and by mid-November 1947, the valley was cleared of all raiders.[13]

In Jammu and Muzaffarabad area, the situation was different. Local population and the Muslim elements in Maharaja's army had risen up against Hindus and Sikhs. Poonch was cut off for nearly one year from the rest of Jammu-Kashmir, but managed to survive because of airforce support. The remaining State troops decided to concentrate on the few towns where members of minority communities from the surrounding areas had taken refuge. All these towns were cut off from one another as well as from Jammu. The history of war in this region therefore is the history of defence of these towns, whose only hope was reinforcement from Jammu or Srinagar. Unfortunately, this expected relief failed to reach them in time except in Kotli and Poonch. Bhimber, Rajauri, Mirpur and Deva-Vatala fell in quick succession.[14]

After the recapture of Uri by the middle of November, the threat to Srinagar had been eliminated, but the situation in Jammu had worsened. The raiders had seized a considerable stretch of territory close to the border with Pakistan. A large number of non-Muslim men had been killed, and their women abducted. According to reports, more than 30,000 non-Muslims had been killed, wounded and abducted when Rajauri was captured by the rebels. Rajauri was recaptured by Indian troops in April 1948 and Poonch by November 1948.[15] By midnight of 31 December 1948, UN-mandated ceasefire came into effect and the areas of Mirpur, Muzzafarabad, Mangala, Kotli, Bhimber etc, which remained under Pakistan's occupation, came to constitute Pakistan-occupied Jammu and Kashmir (POJK).

Events leading to the occupation of Gilgit-Baltistan

The developments in Gilgit-Baltistan need to be studied in greater detail as an impression has been created that the developments in the region in 1947 were independent of happenings in Kashmir Valley and Jammu. It has been also been projected as if the region was liberated by a mass upsurge against the Maharaja's rule, but the truth is that the region was annexed by the Muslim troops of the State Army, who barring a few officers, were not locals. They had been subverted by the same Pakistani propaganda that had afflicted their colleagues in Kashmir Valley and Jammu.[16]

With the lapse of paramountcy in 1947, British Indian Government handed over the administrative control of all areas of the Gilgit Agency, including Hunza, to the Kashmir State Government. Accordingly, Brigadier Ghansar Singh was appointed by the Maharaja as the Governor of these areas on July 19, 1947. When Ghansar Singh accompanied by Major General Scott, the Commander in Chief of State Forces, reached Gilgit on July 30, 1947, he was assured by Major Brown, the Commandant of Gilgit Scouts, its JCOs and other ranks that they would work for the Maharaja if their salaries and service conditions were improved. Similarly, the civil officers too agreed to work with the Maharaja provided their salaries were increased.[17]

As soon as Ghansar Singh took over the administration from the British political agent Lt Col Beacon, on August 1, 1947, the administration came to a grinding halt. This was because all the British officers had opted for Pakistan and the replacements from the State had still not arrived. All the controlled stores were empty and the civilian employees had refused to work till their salaries were increased. General Scott returned to Srinagar on August 2, 1947, with a promise to get some assistance. However, the tense situation in Gilgit fetched no response from the government in Srinagar.[18]

For the next three months, the Governor was a lame duck. Militarily no attempts were made to significantly consolidate the Maharaja's hold in Gilgit agency. One company of 5th Jammu and Kashmir Infantry commanded by Captain Durga Singh and located at Bunji 34 miles short of Gilgit was replaced by 6th Jammu and Kashmir Infantry comprising two companies each of Sikh and Muslim troops and led by Lieutenant Colonel Abdul Majeed Khan. Besides state troops, there were about 500 troops of Gilgit Scouts in the region. They were commanded by Major William Brown, who along with another British officer Captain Jock Matheson, had agreed to serve the Maharaja. Besides these two officers, Captain Mohammad Sayeed Durrani and Lieutenant Ghulam Haider had also been deputed from the State forces to the Gilgit Scouts. After the arrival of the 6th J&K Infantry in the region, the Muslim officers of the State Force established contact with the officers of Gilgit Scouts with the purpose of establishing Pakistani rule in Gilgit.[19]

It must be appreciated that the Gilgit Scouts first was not a homogenous force. Its platoons comprised men from different principalities. In fact the local rulers influenced the populace to a great extent. All the rulers except, the ruler of Chitral professed their loyalty to the Maharaja. In fact, the Raja of Punial had rushed out to defend Ghansar Singh when he was subsequently attacked. Second, the troops were divided along sectarian and ethnic lines. Third, Gilgit Scouts was basically a militia a force that was incapable of taking on the better-armed State forces. The apolitical nature of Gilgit Scouts is evident from their 12-point charter of demands submitted to Ghansar Singh. Its contents relate only to pay and service conditions and nowhere does it talk about Pakistan or any other religious factor. This was the reason why the Governor subsequently chose the Gilgit Scouts to defend Gilgit and not the Muslim troops of state force, who were mainly from Jammu region. It is a fact that most elements from Gilgit Scouts were sitting on the fence and joined the rebels after they had been led to believe that Srinagar had fallen.[20]

Rebellion in Gilgit

After Pakistan invaded Jammu and Kashmir and the Maharaja left Srinagar for Jammu and acceded to India, there was pandemonium in Gilgit. Rumours were thick and strong that Srinagar had fallen. An alarmed non-Muslim population compelled the Governor to send for army detachments from Bunji. The Governor, caught in a bind, chose the Gilgit Scouts over State Forces. On October 30, 1947, he ordered Lieutenant Colonel Majeed Khan at Bunji to reach Gilgit with as large a force as he could muster. However, just after midnight on November 1, 1947, the house of the Governor was surrounded by about 100 Scouts. He yielded to their demand to surrender, ostensibly to protect the lives of non-Muslim residents. The surrender, however, led to the disintegration of State Forces, with large scale killing of troops on the other side of Indus. Most of the Sikh troops were killed; others ran away to the mountains to save their lives.[21]

After the Governor's arrest, a provisional government of 'People's Republic of Gilgit and Baltistan' was set up. It was headed by a local, Rais Khan, and included Major Brown, Captain Ehsan Ali, Captain Hassan (both of State Forces), Captain Sayeed, Lieutenant Haider (both seconded from State Forces to Gilgit Scouts), Subedar Major Babar Khan (of Gilgit Scouts) and Wazir Wilayat Ali. It must be noted that none of the local Rajas were included in the Provisional Government. On November 4, 1947, the Pakistani flag was hoisted at the Gilgit Scouts lines by Major Brown. Brown described his action as a 'coup d'état' and informed Peshawar about the accession of Gilgit to Pakistan. Sir George Cunningham, the new Governor of the NWFP, instructed Brown to restore order. Subsequently, the rulers of Hunza and Nagar, which were vassals of the Maharaja of Kashmir, also declared their accession to Pakistan. The accession of Hunza and Nagar was illegal, as only the Maharaja had the right to accede, and he had already acceded to India.[22]

Major Brown subsequently claimed credit for bringing the region into the Pakistani fold. He was posthumously awarded the Star of Pakistan. However, a careful analysis will indicate that he joined the rebels as a last resort. He and Captain Matheson, another British officer, remained part of the State Army of their free volition and were thus directly responsible to the Governor. Brown also made some attempts to protect the lives of non-Muslim population and was arrested twice by the rebels in the initial days of rebellion but after Pakistan's authority was established, he not only re-established his authority over Gilgit Scouts but also took credit for transferring the region to Pakistan. For Pakistan, it is essential to show that Gilgit Scouts were at the forefront in the rebellion against the Maharaja to portray that the revolt was indeed indigenous - that Brown was moved to action by his troops, local inhabitants, who strongly favoured joining Pakistan. From India's point of view, his involvement indicated British complicity and supported various conspiracy theories.[23]

Chaos and lawlessness was widespread in the Gilgit region for next few days. There was large-scale massacre of Hindus and Sikhs who refused to convert to Islam. It must, however, be noted that the Amirs, Rajas and the people of Gilgit in general had no hand in the revolt or the atrocities perpetrated on the minority community.[24]

Occupation of Baltistan

By the end of November, Pakistan was in complete control of the administration of the Gilgit region. This opened up the way for subsequent Pakistani incursions into Baltistan. This was led by Major Ehsan Ali, another officer from the State Forces and included troops from 6th Kashmir Light Infantry, Gilgit Scouts and about 1200 combatants from Chitral sent by the *Mehtar* of Chitral.[25] The onset of winter and freezing of passes prevented any immediate action.

Baltistan was ruled by a Wazir-i-Wazarat on behalf of the Maharaja who would stay six months in Skardu, three months in Kargil and three months in Laiyya. From 1899 onwards, one platoon with 50 men under a Major or Captain was posted at Skardu, and in Kharpocha Fort, 11 men manned two guns.[26] In 1947, Amar Nath was the Wazir-i-Wazarat of Ladakh and Skardu. He realised that Skardu was probably the weakest link which could possibly be severed by the enemy. He, therefore, moved the administrative headquarters of the district to Skardu. He also selected sites for air strips at Kargil, Ladakh and Skardu, to bring in the army in times of an emergency.[27]

The Siege of Skardu

After the fall of Gilgit and Bunzi, loss of two companies and the imprisonment of the Commanding Officer, the Second-in-Command, Major Sher Jung Thapa, based at Leh, took over the reins of the 6th Battalion. By that time a platoon of State Army under Captain Nek Alam had moved to Skardu from Bunji. Immediately after the fall of Gilgit, Major Sher Jang Thapa was promoted as Lieutenant Colonel and ordered to move to Skardu along with Captain Ganga Singh and 85 Sikh soldiers.[28] Thapa on arrival surveyed the area and wanted to withdraw to Kargil along with the civil administration to set up a firm base there and patrol up to Skardu, but Wazir-i-Wazarat did not approve of his plans. He instead wanted Thapa to set up defences at Stak 70 miles from Skardu and on the border with Gilgit.[29] Thapa eventually selected Tsari 20 miles North West of Skardu towards Rondu to set up his defensive line as it had steep hills on two sides and the River Indus in between.[30]

Tsari was attacked on the night of 8/9 February 1948 and after over-running Tsari, raiders went on to Skardu and launched an attack on the early morning of 11th February, with a well-equipped force of 600, made up of tribals, Chitralis and about 80 deserters of the State Force. The Skardu garrison was able to put up a spirited fight lasting nearly six hours. The Raiders retreated but slaughtered the non-Muslims and ransacked a major part of Skardu town, which was outside the defensive perimeter. The Wazir was killed along with some other Hindu and Sikh officials and the treasury was looted. By the night of February 11, every single Hindu and Sikh at Skardu, which included a large number of women and children, had taken shelter in the cantonment. The retreat by invaders allowed some reinforcements numbering 285 to arrive in Skardu. Still, the size of this force was much too small for undertaking a meaningful defence of Skardu garrison, which also included 229 non-Muslim refugees, 19 Muslim refugees and 22 Muslim civil prisoners.[31]

By the night of 14/15 February, 1948, the siege of Skardu had begun. Major Thapa continued his exertions to stall efforts of the invaders to achieve a breakthrough of his defences, at the same time he kept on requesting for ammunition, supplies and man-power, which were fast depleting. He also suggested withdrawal to Kargil so as to present a much stronger and more compact front. However, the proposal was not approved and the Skardu garrison continued a gallant defence against heavy odds. Few sieges in the annals of modern war have lasted for 185 days, from

11 February to 14 August 1948. The Skardu garrison fought gallantly and ultimately fell when it ran out of ammunition and supplies. The credit for this heroic deed goes entirely to Lt Col Sher Jung Thapa. Without his stand at Skardu, the raiders would have commenced their operations towards Leh earlier and Ladakh could never have been saved.[32]

The fierce resistance and the will to fight exhibited by Skardu Garrison forced them to bypass Skardu and move forward. The rebels supported by Pakistani forces captured Zojila Pass in May 1948 and infiltrated through Drass, Kargil, and other points to threaten Leh. Indian Army had to subsequently use tanks to clear them from Zojila and defend Leh.[33] Leh could only be saved by timely construction of an airfield by an engineer named Sonam Norbu, who created this air bridge with no practical experience and little technical knowledge. With just 13000 rupees and without any bulldozers or mechanical vehicles, he created an airstrip. On 6 April 1948, the airstrip was ready for service. On 24 May, a Dakota carrying Gen Thimayya landed on the airstrip. By July/August, the tribal raiders had been driven back. In November 1948, under Operation Bison, the Indian armed forces reclaimed Zojila and the Kargil area before a cessation of hostilities was announced on January 1, 1949.[34]

UN Resolutions

India made a reference to the United Nations on January 1, 1948 following Pakistan's invasion and illegal occupation of large parts of the state, under a non-binding Article 35 of Chapter VI. A Security Council Resolution of January 17, 1948, called on both sides to "improve the situation" and "to inform the Council immediately of any material change in the situation". On January 20, 1948, it decided to set up a UN Commission for India and Pakistan (UNCIP) directing it to proceed to the spot as quickly as possible. UNCIP arrived in Karachi on July 7, 1948.[35] Based on the UNCIP recommendations, UN passed a resolution on August 13, 1948, which incorporated ceasefire within four days of acceptance of resolution by the two parties. This was to be followed by withdrawal of Pakistani troops, which would be followed by withdrawal of bulk of Indian forces in Kashmir and finally the future of Kashmir will be decided in accordance with the will of the people.[36] The UN Resolution is placed at Appendix A. The ceasefire ultimately came into effect on January 1, 1949.[37]

Present Legal Position

Pakistan refused to withdraw its forces, as required by the UN resolutions, and over the years, radicalisation of population by fundamentalist indoctrination coupled with demographic manipulation in Gilgit-Baltistan has made the reference infructuous. In fact so blatant has been the demographic manipulation in Pakistan that Balwaristan National Movement, a body representing the local population of Gilgit-Baltistan, has even petitioned UN Secretary General Mr Kofi Annan against Pakistan's sinister move to change the demographic character of the area by bringing in Pakhtoons from Khyber Pakhtoonkhwa and

FATA. India waited for several years for Pakistan to fulfil the preconditions for a plebiscite. When that did not happen, the Constituent Assembly of Jammu and Kashmir ratified the accession of the State to India on February 6, 1954. It subsequently adopted a new constitution for Jammu and Kashmir on November 17, 1956, which came into force with effect from January 26, 1957. The Jammu and Kashmir Constitution reaffirms that "the State is and shall be an integral part of the Union of India."[38]

Subsequently, Pakistan attempted to change the Ceasefire Line, by indulging in guerrilla warfare, and accordingly "put the fish in the water to test the temperature" On August 5, 1965, several thousand fully armed Pakistani soldiers in civilian clothes slipped across the ceasefire line. They expected the local population to welcome them but it resisted them and failed their machination.[39] The crushing defeat of Pakistan in 1971 war and the subsequent Simla Agreement was the final nail in the coffin of the already irrelevant UN resolutions. It committed India and Pakistan to resolve all issues peacefully and bilaterally and not to unilaterally alter the situation pending final settlement. India continues to adhere to the Simla Agreement scrupulously.

The Karachi Agreement, April 28, 1949

Pakistan, through the controversial Karachi agreement of 1949, wrested absolute control of Gilgit-Baltistan and consolidated its hold on the occupied areas of Mirpur-Muzaffarabad. The agreement was in complete violation of the UNCIP resolutions. The Agreement was purportedly signed by the Minister without Portfolio in the Government of Pakistan, Mushtaque Ahmed Gurmani, the 'President of Azad Kashmir' Sardar Mohammed Ibrahim Khan, and the Head of the All Jammu and Kashmir Muslim Conference, Choudhry Ghulam Abbas. No person from Gilgit-Baltistan was party or signatory to it, nor did the 'Azad Kashmir' Government have any representation from Gilgit-Baltistan. Further, 'Azad Kashmir' had no historical administrative control over Gilgit-Baltistan, which it could legitimately 'hand over' to the Government of Pakistan. The All Jammu and Kashmir Muslim Conference, moreover, had no political presence in Gilgit-Baltistan. It is difficult to find any legal moral or political authority on whose basis Gurmani surrendered the land and people of Gilgit-Baltistan to an occupying force, without in any way even attempting to seek the concurrence of the people affected by the agreement.[40]

The text of the Karachi Agreement, placed at Appendix B, is quite amateurish and has the form of a memorandum rather than an agreement that aims to politically alter the geography of a disputed region. The most significant component of the 'Agreement' is buried in ambiguous one-liners like 'Matters within the purview of the Government of Pakistan', and 'All affairs of Gilgit – Ladakh under the control of Political Agent'. The future of this strategically significant region and its people was sealed by this single and dismissive phrase, without any further mention of Gilgit-Baltistan in the document. It is pertinent that Sardar

Mohammed Ibrahim Khan has repeatedly, and at various fora, denied being a signatory to the Karachi Agreement.[41] Thus Karachi agreement, which is not only illegal, but also shrouded in mystery allowed Pakistan to consolidate its hold on the Occupied territories of Jammu and Kashmir by delinking Gilgit-Baltistan and creating a façade called 'Azad Jammu and Kashmir'.

NOTES

1. Chaudhri Muhammad Ali, *The Emergence of Pakistan*. New York: Columbia University Press, 1967, pp. 283, 287, 297.
2. Vallabhbhai Patel to Hari Singh, 3 July 1947, in Durga Das (ed), *Sardar Patel's Correspondence 1945-1950: Vol. 1 – New Light on Kashmir*, Ahmedabad: Navjivan Publishing House, 1970, p. 33.
3. Prem Shankar Jha, *The Origins of a Dispute: Kashmir 1947*, New Delhi: Oxford University Press, 2003, pp. 46, 54-58. See, also, Mehr Chand Mahajan, *Looking Back*, New Delhi: Asia Publishing House, 1963, pp. 130, 144.
4. Krishna Menon read out this telegram during his two-day, 8-hour, marathon speech at the UN. Speech on Kashmir at the United Nations Security Council's 762nd Meeting, 23 January 1957. See E.S. Reddy and A.K. Damodaran (eds), *Krishna Menon on Kashmir: Speeches at United Nations*, New Delhi: Sanchar Publishing House, 1992, p. 13.
5. V.P. Menon, *Integration of the Indian States*, Chennai: Orient Longman, 1997, pp. 114, 317-36.
6. S Kalyanaraman, "Dawn of Independence and the Tribal Raid" in Virendra Gupta and Alok Bansal (eds), *Pakistan Occupied Kashmir: The Untold Story*. New Delhi: Manas Publications, 2007, pp. 68-69.
7. Ibid, p. 71.
8. Ibid, pp. 71-72.
9. Parvez Dewan, "A History of POK: Pakistan Occupied Kashmir" in Virendra Gupta and Alok Bansal (eds), *Pakistan Occupied Kashmir: The Untold Story*, New Delhi: Manas Publications, 2007, p. 105.
10. Jha, op. cit., p. 111.
11. Balraj Madhok, *A Story of Bungling in Kashmir*, New Delhi: Young Asia Publications, 1972, pp. 64-68.

12. S. Kalyanaraman, op. cit., pp. 74-75.
13. Ibid, pp. 75-77.
14. Madhok, op. cit.
15. SN Prasad and Dharam Pal, *History of Operations in Jammu & Kashmir (1947–48)*, Ministry of Defence, Government of India, New Delhi, 2005, pp. 49-139.
16. Alok Bansal, "Annexation of Gilgit-Baltistan: Tumultuous Events of 1947-48" in Virendra Gupta and Alok Bansal (eds), *Pakistan Occupied Kashmir: The Untold Story*. New Delhi: Manas Publications, 2007, pp. 85-89.
17. Ibid, p. 87.
18. Ibid, pp. 87-88.
19. Ibid, pp. 87-91.
20. Ibid, pp. 91-92.
21. Ibid, pp. 92-93.
22. Ibid, p. 93.
23. Ibid, pp. 93-94.
24. Ibid, p. 94.
25. FM Hassnain, *Gilgit: The Northern Gate of India*, New Delhi: Sterling Publishers Pvt Ltd, 1978, p. 158.
26. Ahmad Hasan Dani, *History of Northern Areas of Pakistan (Up to 2000 AD)*. Lahore: Sang-e-Meel Publications, 2007, pp. 328-329.
27. S Kumar Mahajan, *Debacle in Baltistan*, New Delhi, 1973, p. 25.
28. Dani, op. cit., pp. 332-333.
29. Mahajan, op. cit., p. 16.
30. Dani, op. cit., p. 371.
31. Ibid, pp. 372-374; Mahajan, op. cit., pp. 55-71.
32. "Operations in Jammu and Kashmir" from Indian Army Website https://indianarmy.nic.in/Site/FormTemplete/frmTempSimple.aspx?MnId=u2z2lTX6FJNOoIkwmbpxGA==&ParentID=d41+/+SDYQLlgTeuB06aiA== (accessed on 27 December 2019).
33. Jasjit Singh, "Battle for Siachin: Beginning of the Third War" in Jasjit Singh (ed), *Kargil 1999: Pakistan's Fourth War for Kashmir*, New Delhi, Knowledge World, 1999, p. 62.
34. Rinchen Norbu Wangchuk, "This Forgotten Engineer Built The Airstrip That Saved Ladakh From Pakistan" from https://www.thebetterindia.com/184059/ladakh-hero-engineer-sonam-norbu-india-pakistan-zojila/ (accessed on 28 December 2019).
35. BG Verghese, "A Jammu and Kashmir Primer: From Myth to Reality", Centre for Policy Research Occasional Paper Series, Occasional Paper No 14, p. 8.

36 Narendra Singh Sarila, *The Shadow of the Great Game: The Untold Story of India's Partition*, New Delhi: Harper Collins Publishers India, 2005, pp. 387-388.
37 Ibid, p. 397.
38 Prithivi Nath Kaul Bamzai, *A History of Kashmir*, New Delhi: Metropolitan Book Company, 1973, p. 798.
39 Ibid, p. 811.
40 Senge H Serring, "Gilgit-Baltistan of Jammu and Kashmir in Constitutional Limbo" in K Warikoo (ed), *The Other Kashmir: Society, Culture and Politics in the Karakoram Himalayas*, New Delhi: Pentagon Press, 2014, pp. 172-173.
41 Ajay Sahni and Saji Cherian, "Gilgit-Baltistan The Laws of occupation", dated 20 May, 2008 from http://intellibriefs.blogspot.com/2008/05/gilgit-baltistan-laws-of-occupation.html (accessed on 27 December 2019).

4

Pakistan Occupied Jammu and Kashmir (POJK)

In previous chapters, we have looked at the historical background and the events of 1947-48 that led to a situation, where significant parts of Jammu and Kashmir came under the control of Pakistan when UN-mandated ceasefire came into effect on 01 January 1949. Administratively, the areas that were part of the State of Jammu and Kashmir and are under Pakistani control are presently divided into two parts and these are the Pakistan Occupied Jammu and Kashmir (POJK) or Mirpur-Muzaffarabad, which Pakistan calls 'Azad (independent) Jammu and Kashmir'. It consists of less than 15 per cent[1] of the land mass under illegal occupation of Pakistan. The area is *Azad* only in name but Pakistan tries to create a facade of autonomy. Then, there is the Union Territory of Ladakh, under Pakistan's occupation, called Gilgit-Baltistan. The region was earlier called

'Northern Areas' of Pakistan, an amorphous entity governed directly by Islamabad and comprises more than 85 per cent[2] of territory under Pakistan's illegal occupation. This chapter will primarily deal with POJK, whereas Pakistan Occupied Territory of Ladakh (POTL) will be covered in the next chapter.

Geography and Administrative Divisions

POJK, which Pakistan calls 'Azad Kashmir', has over 80 per cent of the population of the territory under Pakistan's control as per 2017 Census. POJK has an area of 13,297 sq km and a population of 4.361 million.[3] The territory primarily comprises the Mirpur District of Jammu, the bulk of Poonch, and a portion of the North-Western Kashmir province of the Jammu and Kashmir state, as it existed prior to 1947.[4]

Geographically, POJK, which lies between Latitude 33° and 36° North and Longitude 73° and 75° East, is in Himalayan belt. The terrain therefore is mountainous and hilly, marked by deep ravines. The high mountains in the North form part of Nanga Parbat massif, and encompass Jamgarh Peak at 4734 metres. The northern districts namely, Neelum, Muzaffarabad, Jhelum Valley, Bagh, Haveli, Poonch and Sudhnoti are generally mountainous whereas Kotli, Mirpur and Bhimber in the South are relatively plain. Jhelum River is the main river of POJK along with its two major tributaries, the Neelum (Kishan Ganga) and Poonch, which join Jhelum at Domail and Chomakh, respectively. Mangala Dam, with a capacity of 7.475 million acre feet, stores most of the water of Jhelum to provide irrigation facilities to Pakistan, while submerging the Mirpur town and surrounding areas in POJK.[5] The highest point is Sarwaali Peak at 6326 metres in Neelum Valley,[6] the altitude accordingly varies from 360 metres adjoining Punjab in the South to 6326 metres. The annual precipitation on an average varies from 1000 to 2000 mm. In the north, 30 to 60 per cent precipitation is in the form of snow. The average maximum temperature in winter varies from 20° to 30°C, while the average minimum temperature ranges from 4° to 7°C. The snowline in summer is at 3300 m, but drops down to 1200 m in winters.[7]

Table 4.1: Administrative Divisions with Area and Population

Division	District	District HQ	Area (in Km²)	Population (2017 census)	Languages spoken
Muzaffarabad	Neelum	Athmuqam	3621	191,252	Hindko, Parmi (Pahari version), Kashmiri, Gojri, Shina, Pashto and Kundal Shahi
	Muzaffarabad	Muzaffarabad	1642	650,370	Pahari, Hindho, Gojri and Kashmiri
	Hattian Bala	Hattian Bala	854	230,529	Urdu, Pahari, Gojri and Kashmiri
Poonch	Bagh	Bagh	768	371,919	Pahari
	Haveli	Forward Kahuta	600	152,124	60% Gojri, 30% Kashmiri and 10% Pahari
	Poonch	Rawalakot	855	500,571	Punchhi (Pahari)
	Sudhnoti	Palandri	569	297,584	Pahari, Urdu
Mirpur	Kotli	Kotli	1862	774,194	Pahari
	Mirpur	New Mirpur	1010	456,200	Pahari, Gojri
	Bhimber	Bhimber	1516	420,624	Pahari

Urdu is the official language, but most people in the region speak dialects of Pahari-Pothwari Languages. Gojri is also spoken by nomadic Gujjars. In the north, some people speak Kashmiri and there are isolated villages where Shina and Kundal Shahi are spoken. Currently, the headquarters of the POJK is at Muzaffarabad, which is called the capital of 'AJK' by Pakistan. It is divided into three divisions, namely Muzaffarabad, which constitutes Kashmir part of the territory, Poonch and Mirpur, which together constitute the Jammu part of the territory. These have been further divided into 10 districts and 32 subdivisions.[8] The area, population, languages spoken of all the districts are given in Table 4.1. The details of subdivisions, Union Councils (UCs) and number of villages in POJK are given in Table 4.2.

Table 4.2: Administrative Divisions with Area and Population

Sl. No.	Divisions	Districts				Sub Divisions	
		Name	Sub Divisions	Villages	UCs	Name	Villages
1	Muzaffarabad • 3 districts • 670 villages • 47 UCs	Muzaffarabad	2	415	24	Muzaffarabad Naseerabad	286 129
		Neelum	2	88	9	Athmuqam Sharda	63 25
		Jhelum Valley	3	167	14	Hattian Chikar Leepa	110 33 24
2	Poonch • 4 districts • 14 subdivisions • 412 villages • 63 UCs	Bagh	3	140	20	Bagh Dhirkot Harighel	67 61 12
		Haveli	3	90	9	Haveli Khurshidabad Mumtazabad	39 17 34

Sl. No.	Divisions	Districts				Sub Divisions	
		Name	Sub Divisions	Villages	UCs	Name	Villages
		Poonch	4	122	23	Rawalakot	53
						Haiira	44
						Abbaspur	18
						Thorar	7
		Sudhnoti	4	60	11	Pallandri	27
						Mong	6
						Tararkhal	10
						Baloch	17
3	Mirpur • 3 districts • 11 subdivisions • 686 villages • 73 UCs	Mirpur	2	245	19	Mirpur	176
						Dudyal	69
		Kotli	6	234	36	Kotli	84
						Khuiratta	26
						Charhoi	21
						Darlia Jattan	14
						Sehnsa	71
						Fatehpur	18
		Bhimber	3	207	18	Bhimber	66
						Barnala	94
						Samahni	47
3		10	32	1768	183	32	1768

The map of POJK showing administrative divisions and road links is shown in Map 4.1.

Socio-political Evolution

According to the resolutions of the United Nations, POJK is neither a sovereign state nor a province of Pakistan, but the so-called government of 'AJK' is a 'local authority' with responsibility over the area assigned to it under the ceasefire agreement.[9] This 'local authority' or provisional government of 'Azad' Jammu and Kashmir was established on October 24, 1947 with Trar Khail (Palandri) as its capital and Sardar Mohammad Ibrahim Khan as its President.[10] It

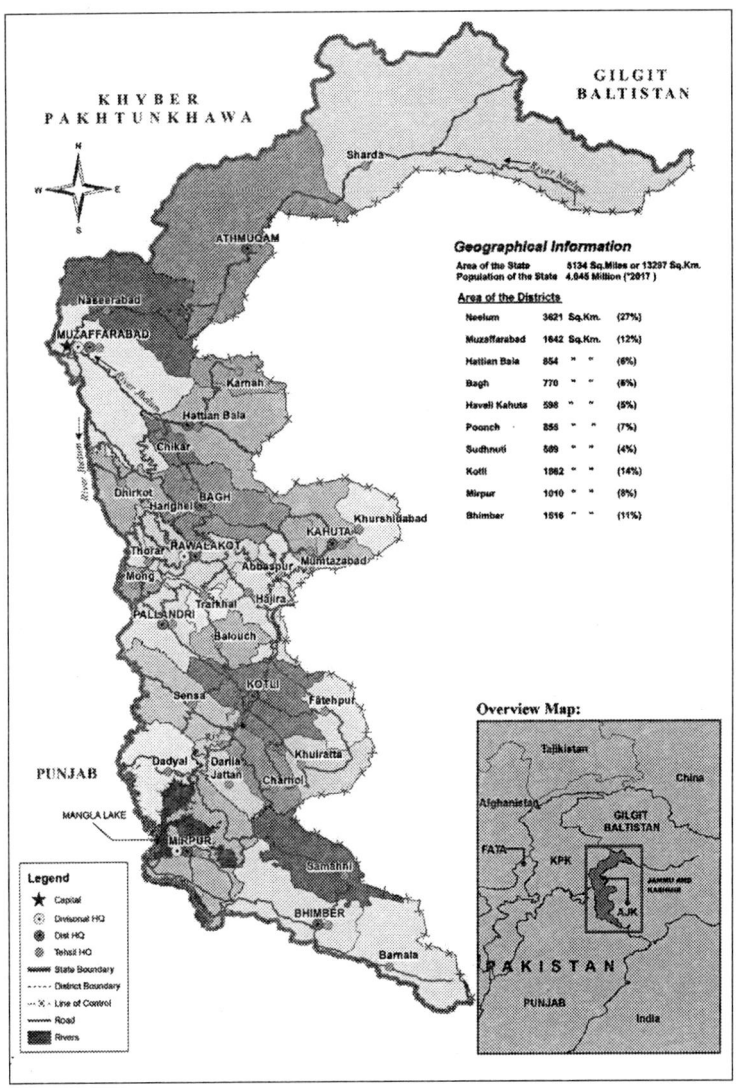

Map 4.1: Pakistan Occupied Jammu and Kashmir
(Administrative Units)

functioned under Rules of Business framed by Pakistan from time to time. The 1949 Karachi Agreement reduced the status of the government of 'AJK' to that of a client state, separated Gilgit-Baltistan and equated a political party, namely, Muslim Conference to the Government. In 1950, for the first time, a semblance of government was provided to POJK, in the form of a President and a council of ministers. It also had a 'Supreme Head', who was defined as the 'Head of Azad Kashmir Movement' and the position was held by the president of Muslim Conference. He appointed the President, who along with his ministers remained responsible to him. In 1952, the rules of business were amended to stipulate that the President will hold office during the 'pleasure of General Council of the All Jammu Kashmir Muslim Conference duly recognised as such by the Government of Pakistan in the Ministry of Kashmir Affairs'. All the authorities were made subservient to the Ministry of Kashmir Affairs based at Karachi.[11]

After Ayub Khan's military coup, a 'Chief Advisor' appointed by the Ministry of Kashmir Affairs became all powerful, and in 1960, when Ayub introduced the partyless Basic Democrat Act, it was extended to the region as well. It created a State Council with 12 members elected by the basic democrats from the region and 12 members selected from the refugees. The Chief Advisor nominated the Chairman of the Council, who acted as the President.[12] During Ayub's rule, the 'President' of AJK, K.H. Khurshid was told to resign by a mid-level police official and was subsequently incarcerated in Palandari and Dalai Camp.[13]

The Basic Democrat Act was replaced in 1964 by an 'AJK' Act, which underwent some were minor changes in 1965, 1968 and 1969. In 1970, the 'Azad' Jammu and Kashmir Government Act was enacted, which for the first time made a provision for a directly elected president. However, the President was required to take an oath affirming his allegiance to POJK's accession to Pakistan, before he could actually take up office. Finally, 'Azad' J&K Interim Constitution of 1974 ushered in parliamentary democracy with Prime Minister as the Chief Executive and an elected assembly. However, the real power vests with 'AJK' Council, which is chaired by the Prime Minister of Pakistan, who also nominates half of its members.[14]

In 1975, when Zulfiqar Ali Bhutto was the Prime Minister of Pakistan, Sardar Muhammad Abdul Qayyum Khan, the then president was suddenly arrested by an officer of Pakistan's Federal Security Forces in Muzaffarabad and subsequently dismissed. Subsequently, when General Zia captured power in a military coup, he sacked the Prime Minister of 'AJK' and appointed Brigadier Muhammad Hayat Khan, a serving officer of the Pakistan Army as the administrator of 'AJK', a post he held for seven years.[15] He was replaced by another military man Major General Abdul Rahman Khan. The office of the Prime Minister remained suspended from 1977 to 1985 under an emergency decree promulgated by the Chief Marshal Law Administrator in Islamabad.[16] After the return to democracy, when Benazir Bhutto was sacked by the President of Pakistan, the Prime Minister of 'AJK', Mumtaz

Rathore, who belonged to Benazir's party, was taken to Islamabad and forced to sign his resignation letter. Subsequently, after General Pervez Musharraf staged a military coup, he sent Major General Sardar Muhammad Anwar Khan as the President of 'AJK', in violation of all norms. Anwar retired just four days before his election and he was retired by an ordinance specially issued by Musharraf, which waived off the two-year restriction on retired government officials from accepting political posts.[17]

The constitution of 1974 with 13 Amendments continues to this date. According to its Preamble, the Constitution was "approved" and its introduction "authorised" by the Government of Pakistan, which tells where power lies.[18] On 06 February, 2018, the Twelfth Amendment to the 'AJK' Constitution was passed declaring Ahmadis as non-Muslims.[19] Subsequently, the Thirteenth Amendment, which was passed on 31 May 2018 and received presidential assent on 01 June 2018, has made large-scale changes in the constitution that further strengthens Islamabad's control over POJK by allowing it to make laws on most important aspects related to the territory, even though it reduces the powers of Kashmir Council drastically.[20]

Myth of Autonomy

POJK or the 'AJK' has all the trappings of an independent state. Its constitution—the Interim Constitution Act of 1974—provides for a parliamentary form of government with a president as the constitutional head, a prime minister as the chief executive, and a 53-member legislative assembly.[21] It also has its own Supreme and High Courts, an election commission, and even its own national anthem and flag. For all practical purposes, however, its administration has traditionally been regulated by Islamabad through its Ministry of Kashmir Affairs and Northern Areas (KANA).[22] Under Section 56 of the Interim Constitution Act (which was drafted in Islamabad by Pakistan's Ministries of Law and Kashmir Affairs), Islamabad has the power to dismiss any elected government in Muzaffarabad, irrespective of the support it enjoys in the Legislative Assembly. The Interim Constitution Act provides for two executive forums: the 'AJK' Government in Muzaffarabad and the 'AJK' Council in Islamabad, which is presided over by the prime minister of Pakistan and exercises paramount authority over the Legislative Assembly. The council from 1974 till 2018 had complete jurisdiction over 52 subjects, which contained virtually everything of significance. Thus, the so-called 'AJK' has no sovereignty of its own and practically functions under Islamabad's direct control.[23] After the Thirteenth Amendment to the Interim Constitution in 2018, POJK has become a de facto province of Pakistan, as most of the powers of the Council have been transferred to the Prime minister of Pakistan.[24]

A total of 12 out of the 45 elected members of the assembly are not elected from the region, but from amongst the refugees residing in Pakistan. Eight members are indirectly elected to the assembly, which include five women and a member each from the technocrats, scholars, and overseas Kashmiris. The region has a dual system of judiciary and the judges in various courts, namely, the Supreme Court, the High Court and the district courts, include Islamic judges acting in accordance with Sharia. These Islamic judges have no legal degree, but deliver judgments on criminal cases involved with Sharia Law. The entire bureaucracy is manned by officers from Pakistan, which include the Chief Secretary, the Finance Secretary, the Inspector general of Police and the Accountant General.[25]

Despite the façade of independence, it is quite clear that the elected leaders of 'AJK' remain completely powerless and act as titular heads, while the real power is vested with the politicians and bureaucrats in Islamabad. Consequently, the regime in 'AJK' invariably changes with that in Pakistan. Islamabad virtually micromanages the administration of the region as all important civil and police posts of POJK are held by officials on deputation from Pakistan, who owe their allegiance to their masters in Islamabad rather than the facile government in Muzaffarabad. The real power in 'AJK', like in Pakistan, is wielded by Pakistan Army and its General Headquarters in Rawalpindi, who deals with the region through its Corps Commander in Murree. The Corps Commander keeps summoning the President, Prime Minister and other officials from the region to give out the army's view on various issues.[26]

The control of Pakistan over the region is so stifling that the oath of office for all, including that for civil servants, includes a pledge to "remain loyal to ... the cause of accession of the State of Jammu and Kashmir to Pakistan".[27] Article 7(2) of the Fundamental Rights chapter provides that "No person or political party ... shall be permitted to propagate against, or to take part in activities prejudicial or detrimental to, the ideology of the state's accession to Pakistan". Similarly, any one contesting an election has to sign a declaration that states, "I solemnly declare that I believe in the Ideology of Pakistan, the Ideology of State's Accession to Pakistan and the integrity and sovereignty of Pakistan".[28] Consequently, nationalist and anti-Pakistan parties that exist are systematically disqualified from contesting elections under this provision. As a result Shaukat Kashmiri, the leader of the United Kashmir People's National Party has been living in exile in Geneva since 1999. Fundamental rights do not apply to actions by defence or other security forces responsible for public order. Freedom of speech is subject to reasonable restrictions in the interests of friendly relations with Pakistan.

Pakistan's constitution is completely silent on the status of 'AJK'. Article 257, which reiterates identical provisions in the 1956 and 1962 constitutions, refers only to the future status of the state: "When the people of the State of Jammu and Kashmir decide to accede to Pakistan, the relationship between Pakistan and that State shall be determined in accordance with the wishes of the people of that State". Pakistan has been unable to remove the ambiguities in its position regarding the constitutional status of POJK because it would not like to do anything that could compromise its demand for a plebiscite in accordance with UN resolutions.[29] Neither has it been able to define its relationship with Gilgit-Baltistan; in 1993, the high court of 'AJK' had passed an order to merge Gilgit-Baltistan with 'AJK'. The order was overturned by the Supreme Court of 'AJK'. However, with the bifurcation of the erstwhile state of Jammu and Kashmir into union territories of Jammu and Kashmir and Ladakh, Gilgit-Baltistan has been shown as a part of Ladakh. 'AJK' will probably have to redefine its relationship with Gilgit-Baltistan.

People, Culture and Languages of Mirpur-Muzzafarabad (POJK)

The population of POJK increased from 2.973 million in 1998 to 4.045 million in 2017. The population figures of both POJK and Gilgit-Baltistan have been kept under wraps by Pakistan authorities. The population growth rate of 1.63 per cent from 1998 to 2017 looks inordinately low, when compared with census figures of 1951, 1961, 1972, 1981 and 1998.[30] This creates an impression that the figures have been manipulated. Although it is often said that almost all the residents of POJK are Sunni Muslims, according to Christian community organizations, there are around 4,500 Christian residents in the region. Bhimber is home to most of them, followed by Mirpur and Muzaffarabad. A few dozen families also live in Kotli, Poonch and Bagh. Most of the Christian population has migrated from Rawalpindi or Sialkot in Punjab province of Pakistan. Consequently, they have been struggling to get residential status and property rights in the region.[31] Recently, the 'President' of

'AJK' accepted their demands for places of worship, education and jobs and said that the government will address them gradually. He also assured them that all hurdles in the path of their getting state subject would be removed.[32] Over 10 per cent of the population of the region in 1947 comprised Hindus and Sikhs, who were relatively prosperous.[33] Most of them were ether massacred or forced to flee. Although a miniscule population of Hindus and Sikhs is believed to have existed in the region, especially in Mirpur, Bhimber and Muzaffarabad districts till 1965, they all either converted or crossed across the LoC. Consequently, there are no Sikhs and Hindus remaining in the region since then. There is no official statistics on the total number of Bahais in the region, although they have been living there before 1947. They had migrated from Iran and many academics, poets, doctors and other professionals of Bahai faith have excelled in different fields. Only six families are now known to be living in Muzaffarabad while some others live in surrounding rural areas. After the passage of Twelfth Amendment, Ahmadis have been added to the list of minorities in POJK. The followers of the Ahmadi faith are estimated to be around 25,000 and most of them live in Kotli, Mirpur, Bhimber and Muzaffarabad.[34]

Though the people of POJK are broadly termed as Kashmiris, most of them have nothing in common with those living in Kashmir Valley so far as culture, clothing or languages are concerned. Most of them identify themselves from their *Biradari* (clan). The ethnic ties of the people are more with Punjab and Jammu than with Kashmir Valley.

Kashmiris are only found in Neelum and Leepa Valleys. Culturally, 'AJK' has similarities with that prevailing in Potohar Plateau of Punjab. Both men and women wear *shalwar kameez* in Pahari style. In addition, women use shawl to cover their head and upper parts of the body.[35] The main Communities are as follows:

> **Gujjars:** They are a tribal community involved in agriculture and pastoralism and are estimated to be the largest community in POJK.
>
> **Sudhans:** Also known as Sadozai, Sardar, they are the second largest tribe, primarily living in the districts of Poonch, Sudhanoti, Bagh and Kotli in Jammu region. They claim their origins from Pakhtoon areas. Sudhans and Rajputs have dominated the political landscape of 'AJK'. Pakistan-inspired rebellion against the Maharaja in Poonch was led by Sudhans.
>
> **Jats:** They are amongst the larger communities of 'AJK' and primarily inhabit the Districts of Mirpur, Bhimber and Kotli in Jammu region. With the inundation of Mirpur city on account of Mangla Dam, a large population of Mirpuris have migrated to UK. It is estimated that the Mirpuri diaspora in the UK is now larger than the population of Mirpuris in POJK.
>
> **Rajputs:** They number over half a million and are spread across POJK. Besides Sudhans, they have dominated the politics of the region.
>
> **Mughals:** A small community located only in Bagh and Muzaffarabad districts.
>
> **Awans:** A clan with significant numbers living primarily in the Bagh, Poonch, Hattian Bala and Muzaffarabad. They also have a significant population in Punjab and Khyber Pakhtunkhwa.
>
> **Abbasis:** A large clan, which resides mostly in Bagh,

Hattian Bala and Muzaffarabad districts. Outside 'AJK', they also live in Abbottabad district of Khyber Pakhtunkhwa and upper Potohar Plateau in Punjab.

Kashmiris: In 'AJK', Kashmiri-speaking population is primarily found in Neelum Valley and in smaller numbers in Leepa Valley in Hattian Bala District.[36]

The official language of the government of 'AJK' is Urdu, although English is widely used in higher echelons of power. Gojri, Kashmiri, Pahari, Pothohari, Hindko, Dogri and Punjabi are widely spoken.[37] Most of the people speak different dialects of Pahari-Pothwari Language Complex and are closely related to both Punjabi and Hindko. Different dialects have been given different names like Mirpuri, Pothwari and Pahari in the South, Chibhali or Punchi in the Centre and Hindko and Parmi in the North.[38] Most of the Gujjars across the region speak Gojri (or Gujari), which is quite similar to Mewati spoken in parts of Rajasthan.[39] In Neelum Valley (and also in Leepa Valley), there is scattered population of people, who speak Kashmiri. They make up the second largest linguistics group after Hindko speakers in the district. Some attempts have been made to promote the teaching of Kashmiri Language, primarily to deny India's monopoly over promotion of Kashmiri culture. However, such attempts have not been successful and even the Kashmiri-speaking residents tend to identify themselves with Urdu rather than Kashmiri. People are gradually shifting towards different dialects of Pahari prevalent in their locality, although there are still some people in Neelum Valley whose mother tongue continues to remain Kashmiri only.[40] In Neelum

Valley, there are three villages where people speak two distinct dialects of Shina, the Dardic language spoken in Gurez and Gilgit as well as some other parts of Ladakh. Pashto, the language spoken in Afghanistan and KP, is spoken in two villages along the Line of Control. In Kundal Shahi village, an extremely endangered Dardic language Kundal Shahi is spoken by around 700 people and is the only language not found outside POJK.[41]

Parties and Politics in 'AJK'

The Muslim Conference, which signed the Karachi agreement, was the only political party permitted in POJK from 1948 to the late 1960s. Despite the party's avowed stance in favour of Pakistan, its leaders often voiced their discontentment over absence of democratic institutions and demanded greater autonomy. However, despite such pretence, the party acted as an extension of Pakistan Muslim League (PML). They not only allowed Pakistan to exercise complete political control over 'AJK' but allowed Pakistan's hand-picked candidates to be installed as the President of the territory. Initially, the President held office at the pleasure of the Party.[42] The next political party, the Pakistan People's Party (PPP-AJK), an extension of Pakistan's PPP, entered the political arena in 1970 and won the first ever legislative elections held in 1975 under the 1974 Act. From then, till 2009 the ruling party in 'AJK' was either the PPP-'AJK' or the Muslim Conference. In 2009, Pakistan Muslim League (N)-'AJK', an extension of Nawaz Sharif's party, gained power and since then power has remained with these three parties. Today there are many other political parties and virtually every major political party in Pakistan from PTI to MQM has an extension in Muzaffarabad. All of them tow the lines of their Pakistani parents and have no separate agendas. As indicated earlier, all parties that oppose Pakistan's control are barred from contesting the elections as the 1974 Act clearly lays down that "no person or party in AJK shall be permitted to propagate against, or take part in activities prejudicial or detrimental to, the ideology of the State's accession to Pakistan". Individuals desirous of contesting elections are required to sign a declaration reaffirming their commitment to Kashmir's accession to Pakistan.[43] Although, political parties are visible symbol of political identification, it is kin-based loyalties that play a major role.[44] These coupled with Pakistan's machinations have undermined the political parties. Islamabad has frequently been accused of manipulating the electoral process in 'AJK' and follows the same pattern as rest of Pakistan.[45]

Pakistani Army and its Terror Camps

The Pakistan Army is the most significant actor in the politics and administration of 'AJK', a consequence primarily of its dominance over the body politic of Pakistan. The hype generated about Jammu and Kashmir in Pakistan's security calculus and its usage to create a state of perpetual hostility towards India have allowed the army to usurp the right to exclusively determine and control Pakistan's Kashmir policy. It has also provided the army the basis of legitimacy for its political role both in Pakistan and in 'AJK'. Pakistan's army perceives control over 'AJK' as critical as it provides

Islamabad a strategic depth in the case of a conventional attack from across the border. Far more significantly, it provides Pakistan with launching pads for militant incursions into Kashmir Valley. The 1949 Karachi Agreement categorically placed the defence and foreign affairs of 'AJK' under Pakistan's control. The 1974 Interim Constitution Act also vested these powers with Islamabad, reinforcing the army's key role in the affairs of 'AJK'.[46]

In the early 1960s, Ayub Khan, who had captured power, actively encouraged sabotage activities across the Ceasefire Line through the Kashmir Public Committee, which was authorized to provide "all out support for guerrillas to be inducted into Kashmir".[47] Around 7000 guerrillas led by special units of the Pakistan army were infiltrated into Jammu and Kashmir with the aim of encouraging revolt in the valley.[48] The revolt never materialized and the misguided operation culminated in the second India-Pakistan war over Kashmir in 1965. The advent of an indigenous Kashmiri uprising against Indian rule in the Kashmir Valley in 1989 provided the Pakistan army with another opportunity for 'liberating' Kashmir. Groups like JKLF received weapons and training from the military's Inter-Services Intelligence (ISI) agency to launch attacks across the LoC. By 1993, the JKLF, which was propagating independence, was sidelined in favour of the Hizbul-Mujahideen, a pro-Pakistan Islamist guerrilla group linked to the Jamaat-e-Islami.[49] As Pakistan gradually expanded the scope of its cross-border militant operations by supporting a variety of jihadi outfits, POJK became a springboard for a low-intensity conflict between India and Pakistan.[50]

Local human rights groups claim that "military intelligence agencies are heavily involved and influential in AJK" and routinely interfere in its politics and governance.[51] Pakistani military installations have often been positioned in close proximity of highly populated civilian areas with an intent to keep a close watch on the population to ensure political compliance and control. Instead of helping to protect the population, the military uses this proximity to often abuse the civilian population.[52] According to Human Rights Watch, a large numbers of Kashmiri detainees are being kept by the Pakistan Army in secret detention facilities in both POJK and Pakistan. Many people have been severely tortured and detained for years; when released, they were barred from returning to their homes and kept in designated areas under constant surveillance. Some of them were militants, but others had no connection with any militant groups.[53]

After militancy took roots in Jammu And Kashmir State in 1989, the situation in POJK transformed rapidly. Militants began to cross into the territory and the government of Pakistan and the 'AJK' authorities welcomed them at that time with a lot of pomp and show, as it gave them a lot of propaganda value. These Kashmiri-speaking militants were culturally and linguistically also distinct from the people of 'AJK' and most of them had no idea of what 'AJK' was beyond a vague awareness that it was "Azad" (free). In 1994, the ISI organized 13 groups operating in Kashmir into the Muttahida [United] Jihad Council. Apart from the Hizbul-Mujahedin, the other members included the

Harkat-ul-Ansar, Jamiat-ul-Mujahedin and Al-Jihad. By early 1999, there were only four or five member groups of the United Jihad Council that were considered effective, including the Lashkar-e-Toiba, Hizbul-Mujahedin, Al Badr and Harkat-ul-Mujahedin. Pakistan Army has been running terror camps in POJK and has been facilitating infiltrations of terrorists in India since 1990s. Any locals or former terrorists who in any way desist from this process are severely punished and tortured.[54]

When a severe earthquake hit POJK in October 2005, the militant groups took over the rescue and relief operations with the active connivance of the Pakistan Army. The army prioritised its own relief work, leaving the civilians at the mercy of militant groups and even tried to mask many of them as charitable organisations. The aim is to build the image of these organisations to facilitate local recruitment.[55] According to Human Rights Watch, the infiltration into Jammu and Kashmir continues unabated, but the locals were extremely reluctant to publicly say so due to the overarching presence of the ISI.[56]

Politics of Water

Mangla dam in Mirpur was built by submerging Mirpur town and its surrounding areas. The water and hydropower from Mangla is supplied to Pakistan, leaving the people of Mirpur high and dry. A majority of Mirpuris have shifted to the UK, but those who remain complain of not receiving adequate compensation for their lands taken for Dam. More significantly, Pakistan is raising the height of the dam to increase the storage for Pakistan agriculture downstream, but in the process inundating more land in the region. Local residents consequently feel discriminated and being exploited economically.[57]

Similarly, hundreds of people protested in Muzaffarabad against Neelum-Jhelum hydropower plant and construction of other dams in the region. They shouted anti-Pakistan slogans and said that the Dam was being constructed to serve the interest of Punjab, while diversion of water had caused grave scarcity. They also wanted a fair share of the power generated by the 1500-MW power plant. Of late, a grave water crisis has engulfed most of POJK, forcing people to live in uninhabitable conditions. Concerned with the grave ecological transformation, people are demanding an immediate rollback of Pakistan's plans of building more dams on Neelum and Jhelum rivers.[58]

Human Right Abuses

Prior to the 2005 Earthquake, 'AJK' was one of the most closed territories in the world. The Pakistani government in Islamabad, the Pakistani army and the Pakistani intelligence services (ISI) practically controlled all aspects of political life in 'AJK'. Although "Azad" means "free", the residents of 'Azad Kashmir' are anything but free; in fact they do not even enjoy basic freedoms of movement or even expression. POJK is a land of strict curbs on political pluralism, freedom of expression, and freedom of association. The press has been completely muzzled. Books even remotely critical of the government are banned.

Arbitrary arrest and detention by security agencies of the local residents as well as torture at the hands of the Pakistani army and the police is fairly widespread. Anyone who wants to take part in public life has to take a pledge of loyalty to Pakistan, while anyone who publicly supports or works for an independent Kashmir is persecuted. Consequently, Kashmiri nationalists who do not support the idea of Kashmir's accession to Pakistan are persecuted. Anyone expressing an independent or 'unpopular' view is targeted by Pakistan Army and intelligence agencies or the militant organizations acting at their behest or independently.[59]

Freedom of expression is tightly controlled; while militant organisations have a free run to disseminate their literature and propagate their views, any one even remotely critical of the government faces its severe wrath. Dissemination of News has been severely limited. Any newspaper or periodical can only be published with an approval from Islamabad and the publisher would have to sign a declaration in support of accession to Pakistan. Journalists are regularly intimidated and consequently resort to self-censorship. Books considered prejudicial to state's accession to Pakistan are banned and that includes all books propagating nationalist discourse. A government officer was suspended for writing a book on Mangla Dam, which was in any case banned for espousing the cause of Kashmiri Rights. Electronic media is totally controlled. After the earthquake, BBC was stopped from telecasting daily "earthquake specials".[60]

Economics of Control

In 1947, apart from Mirpur and Muzaffarabad, POJK consisted of some of the poorest areas in Maharaja's kingdom.[61] However, it boasted significant natural resources, especially for hydroelec-tric power generation. Except for the Mangla Dam, this potential for energy generation has remained underutilized.[62] Even in the case of Mangla, it has been denied royalties of approximately Rs 1 billion ($16.75 million) annually, despite Islamabad's promise of "preferential treatment to 'AJK' in the power tariff" at the time of the construction of the dam in 1967.[63] While the dam caused severe socioeconomic disruption, especially in the Mirpur district, "the benefits of Mangla's electricity were felt in Lahore, and even in Karachi, long before power lines began to be installed in rural Mirpur".[64] Similarly, other potential sources of revenue generation, such as mining of precious stones and tourism, have been neglected. Lack of public and private investment and productive economic opportunities has resulted in substantial migration overseas in search of jobs.[65] But in the absence of a sound investment environment, the potential economic benefits from expatriate remittances have remained untapped.

As a result, POJK continues to be dependent on Islamabad for its developmental and non-developmental budgetary needs. Over the years, Islamabad has plugged POJK's budget deficits with direct injections of grants, but the level of expenditure on socioeconomic development has fallen short of the territory's development needs.[66]

Allocation shortages are compounded by the underutilization of available funds due to the government's limited administrative capacity and poor infrastructure.[67] The economic dependence goes far beyond financial resources, only. Its annual budget is prepared by a centrally appointed finance secretary, and broad economic priori-ties are determined by Islamabad through the 'AJK' council and the chief secretary.

Over the years, the region's economy has been gradually integrated into Pakistan's economy, but this integration has occurred within the context of dependent development, with adverse consequences for the political and economic development of POJK. Cross-LoC trade could help ameliorate some of its economic problems. However, in the absence of economic autonomy, the benefits of such trade are likely to be limited. The earthquake that hit the region on 8 October 2005 has wreaked havoc on the civil infrastructure and has destroyed sources of livelihood and commerce.[68] Although it is too early to predict the impact of economic devastation on the political and economic relations between POJK and Pakistan, one can reasonably speculate that it is likely to exacerbate POJK's traditional economic dependence on Pakistan.

Civil Society in POJK

Economic and political underdevelopment, weak political institutions, and legal restrictions on freedom of association have undermined the development of civil society in POJK and hampered the ability of civil society actors to articulate public interests and demands. Islamabad has frequently used the sensitive nature of POJK to limit the space for democratic forms of contention. For instance, the Maintenance of Public Order Ordinance, which prohibits "activities prejudicial to public safety", is often employed to deter and suppress opposition and dissent. Similarly, press freedoms are severely curtailed. Journalists frequently complain of harassment and intimidation at the hands of intelligence agencies and accuse the government of "using advertisements as an instrument to subdue a hostile press when it criticizes its policies".[69] As a consequence, independent information about politics and government in POJK is conspicuous by its absence.

In an environment where the rights of participation and association are circumscribed, civil society organizations operate in the sanctioned, non-political areas of service delivery, community welfare, and rural development.[70] Islamabad has not been averse to allowing international donor agencies to partner with local organizations for improving health and education facilities, sanitation, rural development, microcredit schemes for women, environmental conservation, refugee resettlement, and related initiatives.[71] Though these efforts have helped address social-sector development deficits within POJK, they have been restricted to projects and programs approved by Pakistan. Hence, local ownership remains low.

While some civil society groups, such as students and bar associations, have occasionally tried to mobilize public opinion through protests and demonstrations,[72] many others derive benefits from the state by espousing pro-Pakistan rhetoric and validating Pakistan's traditional stance on Kashmir. These pro-Pakistan organizations and activists usually represent 'AJK' civil society at both domestic and international forums.

POJK has been a major source of migration to the United Kingdom, the United States, and Canada. Members of the diaspora community have maintained strong social, economic, and political ties with their homeland. Their remittances have been a valuable source of foreign exchange reserves for Pakistan. POJK's legislative assembly has a reserved seat for members of its diaspora community. All major POJK political parties also maintain chapters abroad, which raise funds, rally political support, and try to engage the diaspora community in political developments at home.

Considering the enormous regional and international attention on India-Pakistan conflict over Jammu and Kashmir, internal political and social development in POJK and the nature of its relations with Pakistan have not received adequate academic or policy attention.

NOTES

1. To be exact, 'Azad Jammu and Kashmir' constitutes 13.83 per cent of the land mass of territories under Pakistan's occupation. Source: South Asia 2005 of Europa Publications, 2nd Edition, p. 470.
2. To be exact, 'Gilgit-Baltistan' constitutes 86.17 per cent of the land mass of territories under Pakistan's occupation. Source: South Asia 2005 of Europa Publications, 2nd Edition, p. 470.
3. From "Azad" Jammu and Kashmir Government Website; https://www.ajk.gov.pk/ajk-at-a-glance (accessed on 10 January 2020).
4. Alastair Lamb, Kashmir: A Disputed Legacy 1846-1990, Karachi:

Oxford University Press, 1991, p. 188.
5. "Statistical Year Book 2018", Muzaffarabad: Bureau of Statistics, Planning & Development Department, 'Azad' Govt. of the State of Jammu & Kashmir, pp. 2-3.
6. "AJK Overview" from 'AJ&K' official portal https://www.ajk.gov.pk/ (accessed on 11 Jan 2020).
7. "Statistical Year Book 2018", Muzaffarabad: Bureau of Statistics, Planning & Development Department, 'Azad' Govt. of the State of Jammu & Kashmir, p. 2.
8. https://www.pndajk.gov.pk/uploadfiles/downloads/Statistical%20Book%202017%20Final.pdf.
9. Priyanka Singh, "Political Unrest in Pakistan occupied Kashmir (PoK) - A View from the Pak Press" in K Warikoo (ed.), *The Other Kashmir: Society, Culture and Politics in the Karakoram Himalayas*, New Delhi: Pentagon Press, 2014, p. 256.
10. Parvez Dewan, "A History of POK – Pakistan Occupied Kashmir" in Virendra Gupta and Alok Bansal (ed.), *Pakistan Occupied Kashmir: The Untold Story*, New Delhi: Manas Publications, 2007, p. 107.
11. Smruti S Pattanaik, "How Azad is 'Azad Kashmir': An Analysis of Relations between Islamabad and Muzaffarabad" in Virendra Gupta and Alok Bansal (ed.), *Pakistan Occupied Kashmir: The Untold Story*, New Delhi: Manas Publications, 2007, pp. 163-164.
12. Ibid, pp. 165-166.
13. "'With Friends Like These...' Human Right Violations in Azad Kashmir", Human Rights Watch, Vol. 18, No. 12 (C), September 2006, p. 29.
14. Pattanaik, op. cit., pp. 166-168.
15. Human Rights Watch, op. cit.
16. Dewan, op. cit., pp. 111-112.
17. Human Rights Watch, op. cit., pp. 29-30.
18. Preamble of AJ&K Interim Constitution, 1974; https://law.ajk.gov.pk/assets/lawlibrary/2019-02-13-5c645034ade1415 50078004.pdf (accessed on 10 January 2020).
19. "Ahmadis are not Muslims, decides AJK", *The News*, February 7, 2018.
20. "Azad Jammu and Kashmir Interim Constitution (Thirteenth Amendment) Act, 2018", 'AJK' Government Law, Justice, Parliamentary Affairs and Human Rights Department; https://law.ajk.gov.pk/assets/lawlibrary/2019-02-14-5c647c6b9bfcd1550089323.pdf (10 Jan 2020). Also see, Jalaluddin Mughal, "Who rules Azad Jammu and Kashmir?", *The Friday Times*,

August 17-23, 2018 Vol. XXX, No. 28.
21   The seats were increased from 48 to 53 in 2018 by 13th amendment to "AJK' Constitution.
22   'AJ&K' (AJ&K Interim Constitution, 1974; https://law.ajk.gov.pk/assets/lawlibrary/2019-02-13-5c645034ade141550078004.pdf (accessed on 10 January 2020). The authority of the council has been transferred to Pakistan Government vide 13th Amendment; Human Rights Watch, op. cit.
23   Human Rights Watch, op. cit., pp. 27-28.
24   "Update of the Situation of Human Rights in Indian-Administered Kashmir and Pakistan-Administered Kashmir from May 2018 to April 2019", United Nations Human Rights, Office of the High Commissioner, 08 July 2019, p. 34.
25   Human Rights Watch, op. cit., p. 17.
26   Ibid, p. 29.
27   Ibid, p. 32.
28   United Nations Human Rights, op. cit., p. 35.
29   Asif Ezdi, "Kashmir's legal status", *The News*, July 16, 2009.
30   Bureau of Statistics, Planning & Development Department, op. cit., p. 1.
31   Jalaluddin Mughal, "Unacknowledged existence of minorities in Azad Jammu and Kashmir", Voice of Vienna website; http://voiceofvienna.org/2019/01/08/unacknowledged-existence-of-minorities-in-azad-jammu-and-kashmir/ (accessed on 14 Jan 2020).
32   "Christian community an essential part of our social fabric: AJK president", *The Express Tribune*, January 7, 2020.
33   "Missing Hindus and Sikhs of Pakistan-occupied Jammu and Kashmir"; https://www.dailyo.in/politics/jammu-and-kashmir-pakistan-gilgit-baltistan-hindus-sikhs-1947-partition-karan-singh-poonch-muzaffarabad/story/1/12632.html (accessed on 11 Jan 2020).
34   Mughal, op. cit.
35   Christopher Snedden, *Understanding Kashmir and Kashmiris*. London: Hurst and Company, 2015, p. 9.
36   Human Rights Watch, op. cit, pp. 12-14. Also see, Christopher Snedden, *Kashmir – The Unwritten History*. New Delhi: Harper Collins Publishers India, 2013, pp. 128-133.
37   Bureau of Statistics, Planning & Development Department, op. cit., p. 4.
38   Raja Nasim Akhtar and Khawaja A. Rehman, "The Languages of the Neelam Valley". *Kashmir Journal of Language Research*, Volume

10, Number 1, 2007 p. 68. Also see, Michael Lothers and Laura Lothers, *Pahari and Pothwari: A sociolinguistic survey*. Dallas: SIL International, 2010, pp. 1-4.
39 Calvin R. Rensch et al, *Hindko and Gujari*. Sociolinguistic Survey of Northern Pakistan, Volume 3. Islamabad: National Institute of Pakistani Studies Quaid-i-Azam University and Summer Institute of Linguistics, 1992, pp. 93-100.
40 Tariq Rahman, *Language, ideology and power: language learning among the Muslims of Pakistan and North India*, Karachi: Oxford University Press, 2002, pp. 449-450. Also see, Akhtar and Rehman, op. cit., pp. 70, 75.
41 Akhtar and Rehman, op. cit., pp. 70, 75.
42 Dewan, op. cit., pp. 107-108.
43 Pattanaik, op. cit., pp. 170-171.
44 Leo Rose, "The Politics of Azad Kashmir", in Raju GC Thomas (ed.), *Perspectives on Kashmir: The Roots of Conflict in South Asia*. Boulder: Westview Press, 1992, p. 244.
45 International Crisis Group, India/Pakistan Relations: Steps Toward Peace, Islamabad, Brussels (ICG Asia Report No. 79), 24 June 2004, p. 8.
46 AJ&K Interim Constitution, 1974, op. cit.
47 General K. M. Arif, *Khaki Shadows: Pakistan 1947-1997* Karachi: Oxford University Press, 2001, p. 47.
48 Sher Khan Mazari, *A Journey to Disillusionment* Karachi: Oxford University Press, 1999, p. 129.
49. Sumantra Bose, *Kashmir: Roots of Conflict, Paths to Peace*, Massachusetts: Harvard University Press, 2003, pp. 102-126.
50. Militant groups like Lashkar-i-Taiba, Hizbul Mujahidin, Al Badar Mujahidin, and Harkat-ul-Ansar have received weapons and training to launch attacks across the LoC. Though exact figures are not available, Indian and foreign media reports put the number of training camps along the Pakistani side of the LoC during the 1990s at 91. See Rifaat Hussain, "Pakistan's Relations with Azad Kashmir", in Henry Rowen and Rafiq Dossani (eds), *Peace and Security in South Asia*, Stanford: Stanford University Press, 2005.
51 M. Imran, "Intelligence Agencies Interfering in AJK Affairs, Says HRCP", *Daily Times*, July 20, 2004.
52 Human Rights Watch, op. cit., p. 22.
53 Ibid, p. 52.
54 Ibid, pp. 19-21.
55 Ibid, pp. 22-24.

56 Ibid, p. 8.
57 Ibid, p. 25.
58 "PoK: Protest erupts against Neelum-Jhelum hydropower project", *Business Standard*, July 30, 2019.
59 Human Rights Watch, op. cit., pp. 6-7.
60 Ibid, pp. 32-37.
61 Muzaffarabad was on the main route into the Kashmir Valley until 1947, and Mirpur was the homeland of the Sandans (Muslim Rajputs), who served in large numbers in the Indian army. See Rose, op. cit., p. 237.
62 Built on AJK territory in 1967, the Mangla Dam serves as the principal water storage reservoir for the canal system of West Punjab.
63 Rauf Kalsra, "AJK PM Seeks Islamabad's Help in Settling Power Tariff Row with WAPDA", *The News*, 19 May 2003.
64 Roger Ballard, "Kashmir Crisis: View from Mirpur", in Gull Mohd Wani (ed.), Kashmir: Need for Sub-continental Political Initiative (New Delhi: Ashish Publishing House, 1995), p. 33.
65 Ibid., pp. 28-35.
66 Editorial, "The AJK Budget", *Dawn*, 21 June 2005.
67 "Half of AJK Development Allocation Remains Unutilized", Dawn, 29 April 2004.
68 See Syed Talat Hussain, "Anatomy of a Disaster", *Newsline* (Karachi), November 2005.
69 Human Rights Commission of Pakistan, "State of Human Rights in Azad Jammu and Kashmir: Report of HRCP Fact-finding Mission", July 2004, p. 11.
70 These include government-funded organizations such as the National Rural Support Program (NRSP), locally funded welfare organizations, Pakistan-based non-governmental organizations (NGOs), and externally financed programs and projects.
71 "NGOs Sign MoU to Boost AJK's Poor Households", *The News*, 16 February 2003.
72 Sultan Shahin, "Across the Divide: The Pakistani Model of Freedom", *Asia Times*, 17 December 2004.

5

Pakistan Occupied Territory of Ladakh (POTL)

Administratively, the areas that were part of the State of Jammu and Kashmir and are under Pakistani control are presently divided into two parts. One is the Pakistan Occupied Jammu and Kashmir (POJK) or Mirpur-Muzaffarabad, which Pakistan calls 'Azad (independent) Jammu and Kashmir' and has been covered in the previous chapter. Second is the part of Union Territory of Ladakh, under Pakistan's occupation, called Gilgit-Baltistan. The region was earlier called 'Northern Areas' of Pakistan, an amorphous entity governed directly from Islamabad and comprising more than 85 percent[1] of territory under Pakistan's illegal occupation. As brought out earlier, from 31 Oct 1947 onwards, till the UN-mandated ceasefire of 1 Jan 1949, Pakistan kept on attacking areas of Ladakh. The initial rebellion was led by the subverted elements of

Maharaja's Army and supported by Gilgit Scouts. They were later joined by the Pakistan Army and troops from Chitral.

Till 1901, Gilgit, Baltistan and Ladakh were all a part of a single administrative division called Northern Frontiers. Post 1901, to face the challenges of an assertive Russia, northern frontiers were divided into Wazarats of Gilgit and Ladakh (which included Baltistan). After the recent reorganisation of the state of Jammu and Kashmir into union territories of Jammu and Kashmir, and union territory of Ladakh, the boundaries of Ladakh virtually reflect pre-1901 boundaries.

Gilgit-Baltistan, a region of over 72,000 square kilometres, is an area that has historically been of pivotal strategic importance. It is the ancient 'axis of Asia', where South, Central and East Asian commerce converged. Being at the crossroads of three great civilizations, it has been often described as the point "where three empires meet". Gilgit-Baltistan has been traditionally both India's and Tibet's gateway to Central Asia and beyond, into the heart of Europe, along the ancient Silk Route that contributed so much to the wealth and civilisation of Bharat. The loss of Gilgit-Baltistan has resulted in India's 'encirclement' and its containment within the South Asian region. [2]

The blocked access to Central Asia has imposed increasing geo-strategic costs, as India looks to engage with the emerging republics of Central Asia, and the markets of Europe via land routes. China is engaging with the Central

Asian Republics to create a 'land bridge' to Europe. For India, economic viability of a wide range of Indian exports, and the competitiveness of significant sectors of the Indian economy, depends on securing comparable land access. This land access is occupied by Pakistan, which has blocked transit of Indian humanitarian aid to Afghanistan. By occupying Gilgit-Baltistan, Pakistan has driven a permanent wedge between India and the people of Khyber Pakhtunkhwa, who under the leadership of the 'Frontier Gandhi', Khan Abdul Ghaffar Khan, wanted to be a part of India in 1947. By occupying Gilgit-Baltistan, Pakistan has managed to create an overland access to China, which has enabled a Sino-Pak nexus to develop and has led to ceding of Shaksgam valley and trans-Karakoram tracts by Pakistan to China.[3]

The Land and the People

The region, which is a mountainous landmass of slightly less than 73,000 km^2 and straddles parts of Karakoram, Hindukush and Himalayan ranges, is home to the longest glaciers outside the polar region and some of the tallest peaks in the world, including K2, the second highest peak in the world. Presently, the region is divided administratively, into three Divisions, namely, Gilgit, Diamer and Baltistan. These are further subdivided into ten districts. Gilgit division comprises four districts, namely Gilgit, Ghizer, Hunza and Nagar, whereas Diamer Division has two districts Diamer and Astore. Baltistan Division consists of Skardu, Shigar, Kharmang and Ganche districts. The area and population of various districts are as follows:

Table 5.1: Area and Population of Districts and Divisions of Gilgit-Baltistan[4]

Division	District	District HQ	Area (km^2)	Population (2013 est)	Remarks
Gilgit	Gilgit	Gilgit	14,672	222,000	
	Ghizer	Gahkuch	9,635	190,000	
	Hunza	Aliabad	7,900	70,000 (2015)	Area of Shaksgam Valley, 5,180 km^2 has not been included
	Nagar	Nagar	5,000	51,387 (1998)	
Diamer	Diamer	Chilas	10,936	214,000	
	Astore	Eidgah	5,092	114,000	
Baltistan	Ghanche	Khaplu	4,052	108,000	The area shown by Pak authorities includes Siachin Glacier
	Kharmang	Kharmang	5,500	305,000 (1998)	Combined population of the three districts in 1998
	Shigar	Shigar	8,500		
	Skardu	Skardu	8,700		

In April 2019, the cabinet of Gilgit-Baltistan announced creation of four new districts. Accordingly, creation of Gupis-Yasin District in Gilgit Division, Darel and Tangir Districts in Diamer Division and Roundu District in Baltistan Division, has been announced. The district infrastructure, however, is in the process of being set up and districts should start functioning fully by mid-2020.

GB is surrounded by Uyghur Autonomous Region of Xinjiang, Wakhan Corridor of Afghanistan, Chitral and

PAKISTAN OCCUPIED TERRITORY OF LADAKH (POTL)

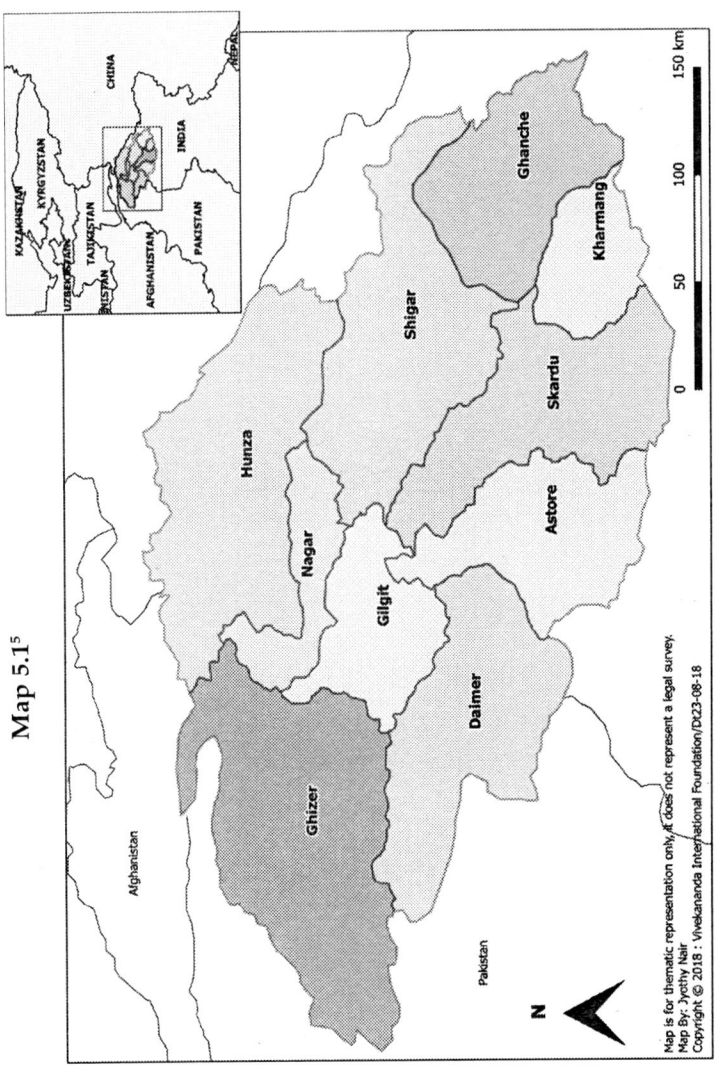

Map 5.1[5]

Kohistan districts of Khyber Pakhtunkhwa, POJK and other parts of the Union territories of Jammu and Kashmir and Ladakh. The region is also home to the world's second highest plateau, the Deosai plains, with an area of 5,000 km^2. The climate of the region is very diverse with many rain shadow areas. Gilgit and Chilas towns are hot in summers while cold in winters, while valleys of Astore, Khaplu, Yasin, Hunza and Nagar are even cold in summers. Eastern regions of Himalayas are moist but western regions of Karakoram are dry. Most valleys have desert-like climate.[6]

The region has enormous ethnolinguistic diversities. In Dardistan, where people are racially Aryans, the population has traditionally been divided into four castes: Shins, Yeshkuns, Kamins and Doms. Shins are the elites and Yeshkuns are landowners, Kamins on the other hand are low-caste tenants and craftsmen, whereas Doms are musicians and Blacksmiths.[7] They speak various Indo-Iranian languages like Shina, Khowar, Wakhi, Domaaki and Kohistani, which are interrelated and most of them belong to the Dardic group of languages. In addition, Burushaski, a language isolate, is also spoken in Yasin, Hunza and Nagar Valley of Gilgit region.[8] All these languages are without standard scripts and are spoken by very small groups of people. On the other hand, people in Baltistan, who belong to the Tibeto-Mongoloid stock speak Balti (a dialect of Ladakhi, a language of Tibetan group, which originally had a Tibetan script and which has since been replaced by Persian script).[9]

The population is Islamic but with varying sectarian

orientations that imbibe pre-Islamic customs and beliefs. In Hunza, Ismaili beliefs are prevalent; in Nagar and Eastern Gilgit people follow Twelver Shia Islam. Down South, near Shinkari, people follow Sunni Islam. In Baltistan, most people follow Twelver Shiaism while a minority adhere to Nurbakshi Sect, who consider themselves distinct from both Shias and Sunnis and inhabit North and South-Eastern part of Baltistan.[10]

The population of the region comprises numerous ethnic groups and tribes and is believed to have grown by 63.1 percent from 883,799 in 1998 to 1,441,523 in 2011, whereas the number of households has increased by 49.9 percent from 109,318 to 163,887 during this period according to the preliminary results of house listing as part of 2011 Census.[11] In terms of population growth since 1998, the annual growth rate in Gilgit-Baltistan stood at 3.81, much higher than the population growth in Pakistan. This fact coupled with the fact that the maximum increase in households was observed in Gilgit and Diamir districts gives credence to the allegations that a large number of outsiders, primarily from KP have settled in these districts, which are connected by Karakoram Highway.[12] The issue has been so sensitive that the 2017 census figures for the region have not yet been published, although it has been done for POJK and all the provinces of Pakistan.[13]

The Economic Potential

The region has its unique flora and fauna and abounds with exotic wild animals and birds, which are rare in other parts of the world. Markhors (ibex), Marko Polo sheep, snow tigers, leopards, oxen, snow bears, eagles, vultures, kites, red-legged partridges, tohchons, choughs, pygmies and so many other birds are found in this region. There are thick forests in the Dardistan, which cover almost 11,000 hectares of the land. Most of the Gilgit valley is well cultivated, with fruit trees in the fields. Wheat and barley are grown and where water is available, there are fairly good crops of rice, but where cultivation has not been attempted, the land is barren, though some of the hills carry large woods of fir and juniper, and at higher reaches there are birch trees.[14]

Conifer forests of Chir pine abound in Baltistan along the stream of Basho and Rondu. The region is rich in mineral resources and produces a number of precious metals and important radioactive materials. The region has huge reserves of gold and a number of gold mines exist especially in Bashah, Braldo, Parkuta, Saltoro and in the rivers of Shigar, Indus and Shyok. Good quality marble is mined in Kwardo near Skardu, whereas black marble is found in Gulabpur and Chotron. In fact the entire stretch of land from Kwardo to Basha is full of marble. In Wasoned in Shigar valley, emerald is mined and a mica mine exists near Nyaslo stream in the Basha Valley. Copper sulphate is mined in Chorbat. Iron mines exist in Nend in Shigar and Chotron in Braldo, whereas lead is mined in Pharda in Khapulu and Daso in Shigar. Antimony is found in the area of Stak in Rondu and Alum is found in Ghowari stream and in Ashkopo.[15] In addition, the region has mines of Uranium 238, ruby, topaz, quartz, iron, sulphur and oil.[16]

Ruby, emerald, topaz, aquamarine, fluorite, and lapis-lazuli gems are also found in the valleys of Gilgit and Hunza.[17]

The economy in Dardistan is based on agriculture in irrigated terraced fields and rearing of animal herds on high mountain pastures in summer and stall feeding in winters. Maize, wheat and barley are the main crops, although some rice is also cultivated at the bottom of some valleys. Millets, lentils and certain kinds of beans are sowed in middle and higher fields, while buckwheat is cultivated in the highest fields. Mulberries, apricots, grapes and other dried nuts are popular fruits, whereas peaches, cherries, apples and figs are grown in regions which have contact with outside world; very few green vegetables are known to the local population. In narrow valleys, with small patches of arable land, a system of community transhumance is practised. People first sow the fields where two crops are feasible, and then move to the higher fields where only one crop is feasible. Some of them then move to higher meadows with cattle, whereas the rest return to the bottom to harvest the crop and sow again. In autumn when the herdsmen move down with the cattle, they harvest the crop in higher fields first and then the lower fields. In broader valleys, with large arable land, the soil has been divided amongst communities, which have fields around them. They usually have two crops and do not indulge in transhumance; only the unmarried shepherds take the cattle up to the higher pastures. In some valleys like Tangir, where climatic conditions are excellent, the entire agricultural work is done by tenants, whereas the original population moves to higher reaches. Hunting, which was an important source of sustenance in the past, is now merely a sport and fishing is of no significance. Craftsmen are paid for by grants of land or food grains, but most of these works are now being done by tenants to augment their limited income. Most of the wares are imported from the markets of Gilgit, Chilas or Mingora. Weaving and tailoring are done exclusively by men.[18]

Baltistan on the other hand is a desert like Ladakh, with hardly any precipitation; as a result no agriculture is possible without irrigation. However, Baltistan is at a lower altitude with respect to Ladakh and is therefore slightly warmer; it also receives scattered snow and rainfall in some places. The valleys of Shyok River and Indus River are under cultivation. Rabi crops sown are wheat, gram, peas, pulses, beans and rapeseed. During Kharif season millets, buckwheat and coarse grains are grown. Rice and maize are not grown and attempts to introduce them have not been successful. Good quality vegetables are grown, which include spinach, turnips, chillies, horse radishes, carrots, onions, cauliflower and potato. Watermelons, melons and cantaloupes are available in abundance. Mild climate supports growth of fruits. Mulberries, apricots, plums, peaches, apples, pears, grapes, redcurrants and walnuts are grown extensively. Grapevines are not grown on stakes but made to climb the mulberry trees. Almond, introduced during the Dogra rule, also grows well in the region, but is still not very popular. Pomegranates are grown in the lower regions. There is hardly any industry in the region, but some woollen shawls and garments are manufactured in parts of Baltistan. Large quantity of apricot and its kernel are exported. By and large, the people are poorer than their brethren across the Line of Control in Kargil and Ladakh.[19]

Geopolitically, it is one of the most sensitive areas of Pakistan and has assumed additional political and strategic importance with the opening of the Karakoram Highway,[20] which links China to Pakistan and reportedly generates trade worth billions of dollars. The region used to be a major tourist destination till Pakistan went nuclear in 1998, and tourism was a major source of employment in the region. However, Pakistan's nuclear tests along with terrorist attacks on World Trade Centre, have almost dried up this avenue. Despite large-scale publicity, only 4,000 foreign tourists arrived for K2 Golden jubilee celebrations in 2004.[21] The resultant unemployment and lack of opportunities have created an explosive situation and have led to widespread unrest and frustration amongst the masses.[22] However, it is still the most sought after tourism destination in entire Pakistan and areas under its occupation. According to official estimates, some 80 percent foreign tourists coming to Pakistan visit the region every year.

Despite being a rain-deficit region, the region has enormous water resources as almost all peaks are covered with heavy snow in winter. Water flows in summer due to melting of mighty glaciers. Other water sources are the beautiful natural lakes, flowing into rivers and giving birth to the famous Indus River, which irrigates Pakistan. Less than 10 percent of the hydroelectric potential of the region has been tapped for local use.[23] This especially is ironic as

Pakistan intends to build megadams at Skardu and Bhasha, which will inundate millions of acres of populated fertile lands to provide cheap electricity to Pakistan.

Northern Areas

Since 1947, the region has been treated by Pakistan's rulers as a virtual colony. Local residents were denied any role in their own governance and were governed under barbaric Frontier Crimes Regulations, enacted by the colonial masters to subdue recalcitrant tribes in Federally Administered Tribal Areas (FATA). Even the historical identity of the region was diluted by naming the region as 'The Northern Areas'. Till 1967, an official sitting in Karachi, thousands of miles away from Gilgit-Baltistan, lorded over the destiny of its residents. To compound matters, Pakistan gave away 5,180 km^2 of its territory to China as part of Sino-Pak Agreement on 02 March 1963. The agreement is placed at Appendix C. In 1967, Pakistan created a post of Resident based in Gilgit, and in 1969 for the first time a local elected body 'Northern Areas Advisory Council' was established, with purely advisory functions. In 1971, India managed to retake approximately 804 km^2 of territory in Gilgit-Baltistan. This was followed up with firm military actions to prevent Pakistan from occupying the Siachen Glacier and surrounding regions in 1984. Pakistan perceives that India captured 3,000 km^2 of territory in the region.[24]

Northern Areas Advisory Council initially transformed into Northern Areas Council and finally into Northern Areas Legislative Council (NALC) by 1999. However, all these bodies remained mostly advisory with extremely limited legislative power.[25] Growing pressure from the local population eventually forced Pakistan to grant them a modicum of self-governance and Gilgit-Baltistan (Empowerment and Self-Governance) Order 2009 was promulgated by the then Pakistani President Asif Ali Zardari. The order renamed the region as Gilgit-Baltistan, a long-standing demand of the residents. It also gave the region its own Chief Minister, Governor and judiciary. However, all these organs were in reality powerless and the real power remained with Islamabad. More significantly, by giving the region structures similar to a Pakistani province, Islamabad has attempted to amalgamate this region into Pakistan.[26] Finally, in 2018, Pakistan introduced Gilgit-Baltistan Order 2018, superseding the 2009 order, even though the Supreme Appellate Court of Gilgit-Baltistan had struck it down.[27] With the implementation of G-B Order 2018, Pakistan has converted this region into a de facto Pakistani province.

Discontentment with Pakistan

There has been huge discontentment in Gilgit-Baltistan against Pakistan's occupation. People have accordingly been protesting against it for decades. The main causes of the discontent are the absence of political rights, where the local residents for decades had no institutions of self-governance and even today the elected representatives have no real powers. More significantly, for contesting the elections, one has to profess unflinching loyalty to Pakistan. To compound matters, Islamabad has been trying to change the demography of this strategic region. State Subject Rule, which was imposed by the Maharaja of Jammu and Kashmir to prevent outsiders from becoming naturalised citizens of the state, was abrogated in 1974 for Gilgit-Baltistan by Zulfiqar Ali Bhutto, which opened the floodgates for outsiders to move into this pristine region. Consequent change in demography has also affected the delicate sectarian balance as the number of Sunni members in the Legislative Assembly has increased significantly.[28]

General Zia ul Haq, who usurped power from Bhutto, introduced and promoted Sunni Deobandi Islam in this Shia majority region, which has led to sectarian tensions. Construction of Karakoram Highway made this region accessible and brought in Sunni extremist outfits like Sipah-e-Sahaba, which tried to impose their radical ideology in the region, which was opposed by the Shias, both Twelvers and Ismailis and Nurbakhshis. This culminated in Shia-Sunni and Shia-Nurbakhshi riots in Skardu, leading to grave sectarian polarisation. The realisation that the Pakistani State was supporting these Sunni outfits led Shias to come out in large numbers to violently protest in Gilgit in May 1988. The fact that Shias celebrated Eid, while Sunnis were still fasting led to a major riot.[29] In retaliation, Sunni tribesmen from Khyber Pakhtunkhwa[30] and FATA descended on the region and burnt homes and crops and killed hundreds of Shias.[31] Since then, sectarian riots have become a regular feature with Shias at the receiving end. Whenever the local residents demanded self-governance, the riots were engineered to divide them.[32]

During Kargil War, Laskar-e-Taiba was given a free hand in the region by Pakistan's military establishment, which exposed the region to its rabidly anti-Shia ideology and resulted in greater polarisation and hardening of positions. In 2003-04, Shias objected to the contents of Urdu and *Islamiyat* text books as being contrary to their religious beliefs.[33] Popular discontentment forced the authorities to close all educational institutions for one full academic year till April 2005, and open them only after all controversial portions had been removed. Imam Aga Syed Ziauddin Rizvi, the local Shia cleric, who helped the authorities to resolve the issue, was shot by Sunni extremists in Gilgit on January 8, 2005. He finally succumbed to his injuries and his death led to riots that continued for weeks and thereafter kept erupting from time to time. The riots even claimed the life of the Inspector General of Police, the senior most police officer of Gilgit-Baltistan.[34]

The sectarian violence has continued unabated since then, and buses plying on Karakoram Highway and specifically the Shia passengers in them have been attacked regularly. In September 2009, a bus carrying Shias from Baltistan was torched by Sunnis. On 28 February 2012, unidentified gunmen forced passengers to disembark from four Gilgit-bound buses and killed 18 Shia passengers. In August 2012, 25 Shia passengers were pulled out from three buses and shot, with Tehrik-e-Taliban Pakistan (TTP) taking responsibility for the killing. In 2013, terrorists from Junood ul Haifa, a new wing of TTP, killed 10 foreign tourists and their local Shia cook at the base camp of Nanga Parbat at an altitude of 4,200 m. The growing footprint of TTP in the region has further aggravated the sectarian faultlines.[35]

The local population in Gilgit-Baltistan has been protesting against Pakistan's occupation for last few decades; however, it has failed to receive the requisite support from the Indian government or the international community. Even the Indian public is generally unaware of the sufferings of these people, who are constitutionally and legally citizens of India. The reasons for their alienation are many, which stem from lack of representation in various organs of the government, absence of self-governance, ethnic and sectarian marginalisation to economic exploitation. However, the most significant reason for their discontentment is the belief that their unique cultural and linguistic identity is getting extinguished under the sustained onslaught of radical Islamist forces. People perceive that Pakistani authorities are deliberately trying to obliterate their ethno-linguistic and cultural identity. As the number of people speaking different languages is rather small, the influx of outsiders threatens the very survival of these languages in the absence of suitable institutional support. These languages are hardly taught anywhere and it appears as if Pakistani state wants the unique cultural identity of this region to get subsumed within the overall Islamic identity of Pakistan. The people are therefore agitated as they feel that their rich cultural heritage will be lost forever.[36]

It is essential that Indians know about the sufferings of these people and their unique and rich pre-Islamic culture and languages, which have withstood the onslaught of time. The population of Gilgit-Baltistan looks towards the government of India and its masses to provide them moral support in their quest for political rights and freedom from Pakistan's brutal and oppressive rule.

Strategic Importance of Gilgit-Baltistan for India

The occupation of Gilgit-Baltistan cuts off India's access to existing trade routes via Gilgit. The region shares its borders with Tibet, Pakistan, Afghanistan, Xinjiang (East Turkestan), and through them with Central Asian Republics and other parts of the Union territories of Jammu and Kashmir and Ladakh. It was historically India's gateway to Central Asia and was the centre of trade routes to China, Persia and beyond. With this region, India could have had borders with Afghanistan and Tajikistan, a Central Asian Republic, would have been just 25 km away. This territory is the meeting point of trade from West Asia, Central Asia, South Asia and East Asia. Gilgit to Iran is 1,000 km by road, which is around the same distance between Gilgit and India's capital New Delhi. Gilgit to Russia's capital Moscow is 3,500 km by road. Comparatively, that distance is just 300 km more than Gilgit to Chennai in south India by road.[37] Thus Gilgit-Baltistan is an extremely important point connecting many regions of Asia with Europe, by land. Trade routes are the routes for military too, and often armies use existing trade routes.

Pakistan and China built the Karakoram Highway that connects Gilgit to Kashgar. From Gilgit, existing Pakistani highways connected landlocked Xinjiang to Arabian Sea. Three central Asian republics, namely, Uzbekistan, Kazakhstan and Kyrgyzstan, are in talks with China to connect to Karakoram Highway via Kashgar and get access to Arabian Sea. China-Pakistan Economic Corridor (CPEC), a key component of China's ambitious Belt and Road Initiative (BRI), intends to re-create ancient Silk routes in Asia. CPEC enters into Gilgit-Baltistan through Khujerab Pass, creating a land route from Xinjiang to Gwadar port in Balochistan.

Gwadar port access cuts down the distance from Xinjiang to the Arabian Sea to merely 2,500 km. Today Xinjiang is 4,500 km away from the East coast of China. The CPEC project has the Karakoram Highway at its heart, as China can access Gwadar port only via the Kashgar Gilgit Highway, which has to transcend through Pakistan Occupied Territory of Ladakh (POTL) – the Gilgit-Baltistan.

Security Concerns for India

All conventional conflicts between Pakistan and India post-1971 have been confined to the Line of Control in Union Territory of Ladakh. In 1984, Indian Armed Forces fought Pakistan Army, under Operation Meghdoot, to pre-empt Pakistan's attempts to militarily occupy Siachen Glacier. Kargil War in 1999 was also started in the region when Pakistan's army crossed the Line of Control from Baltistan and occupied high peaks in the Kargil region.

With the centrality of the region in China's future plans of making CPEC economically viable, its investments in the region have been consistently increasing. China has deployed more than 3,000 troops in this area to guard its workers and physical assets. In 2017, for the first time ever, Chinese troops participated in Pakistan Day Parade and marched in Islamabad. As part of CPEC, China has already taken over the Gwadar Deep Sea Port and is believed to be setting up naval facilities. These are the events that have a profound impact on security of India. One of India's avowed objectives is not to internationalise the Kashmir Issue, but it has become inevitable with China, Pakistan and CPEC, coming into it.[38]

Siachen, the highest battleground in the world, is sandwiched between three nuclear armed nations: India, Pakistan and China. The strategic Saltoro Ridge overlooks Gilgit-Baltistan to its west and has to be crossed by anyone seeking access from Skardu to the Karakoram Pass. Any Pakistani presence in Karakoram would be a threat to India in Ladakh from the north in addition to Chinese locations in Aksai Chin. Siachen being in the possession of Pakistan would have given it access to the Karakoram Pass from Skardu and eventually linking it with Shahidullah on the Kashgar-Shigatse road that runs parallel to the Tibet-India border. Indian troops today control most of the glaciers and access the region through the world's highest motorable road at Khardung La with a helipad at a place called Sonam, at 21,000 feet.[39]

Water Concerns for India
The inauguration of Bhasha Dam by General Pervez

Musharraf on April 26 2006 has caused immense consternation in the region as it will inundate large tracts of land in Diamer district of Gilgit-Baltistan. In addition, Pakistani establishment has also proposed the construction of a huge 35 million acre feet dam at Skardu, which will submerge the entire Skardu bowl, the hub of Balti cultural heritage. The Baltis feel that the proposed dam is nothing but an attempt to bulldoze and subdue the already poor and marginalised Baltis in Skardu.[40] There has been large-scale opposition to the proposals for the construction of the dam. Even Kashmiri outfits like Jammu and Kashmir Liberation Front (JKLF) have come out strongly against the dams and have demanded that Bhasha Dam be named as Diamer Dam and all the royalty from the dam should come to Gilgit-Baltistan.[41]

Now after more than a decade, China is looking at building of massive dams in Gilgit-Baltistan, referred to as the North Indus Cascade. The North Indus Cascade is envisaged to originate in Skardu in Baltistan before flowing into Khyber Pakhtunkhwa with an installed capacity of about 22,230 MW of hydropower. The string of projects includes 7100 MW Bunji Dam, 4500 MW Diamer Bhasha Dam, 4320 MW Dasu Dam, 2400 MW Patan Dam and 4000 MW Thakot Dam. China and Pakistan hope to harness at least half of Indus River's estimated hydropower potential of about 40,000 MW. Chinese have committed $50 billion towards the North Indus Cascade, which is the second largest Chinese commitment towards Pakistan after CPEC. Apart from providing Pakistan with low-cost power, the range of dams are also expected to act as silt trap for the Tarbela dam, which is currently Pakistan's largest dam and its capacity is getting reduced due to increased siltation. The project is obviously opposed by India, as it infringes upon India's territorial sovereignty as projects are being planned on what is de jure Indian Territory.[42] Gilgit-Baltistan also contains three largest glaciers outside the Polar Regions. These glaciers are huge sources of fresh water, but due to Pakistani occupation, these fresh water reservoirs are outside India's reach.

There have been large-scale protests against the dams in this region. People are concerned about the ecological impact of such megadams in a tectonically fragile region. The students in Gilgit-Baltistan have also been asserting that Chitral and Kohistan in Khyber-Pakhtunkhwa are historically part of Gilgit-Baltistan and were separated from it by Pakistan as part of a conspiracy. They have also emphasized that the region is a disputed territory and Pakistan should not build a megadam without resolving its status.[43] These newer and growing demands are nothing but manifestation of increasing alienation of the population from Pakistan.

NOTES

1 To be exact, 'Gilgit-Baltistan' constitutes 86.17 per cent of the land mass of PoK. Source: South Asia 2005 of Europa Publications 2nd Edition, p. 470.
2 Ajai Sahni and Saji Cherian, "Gilgit-Baltistan The Laws of Occupation", Intellibriefs, May 20, 2008; http://intellibriefs.blogspot.com/2008/05/gilgit-baltistan-laws-of-occupation.html (accessed on 10 January 2020).
3 Ibid.

4. Alok Bansal, *Gilgit-Baltistan and its Saga of Unending Human Rights Violations*, New Delhi: Pentagon Press LLP, 2018, pp. 29-30.
5. Ibid, p. 31.
6. Ibid, 29-33.
7. Karl Jettmar, *Bolor & Dardistan*, Islamabad: National Institute of Folk Heritage, 1980, pp. 35-41.
8. Stephen Philip Cohen, *The Idea of Pakistan*, New Delhi: Oxford University Press, 2005, p. 209.
9. Tariq Rahman, *Languages and Politics in Pakistan*, Karachi: Oxford University Press, 1998, pp. 217-222.
10. Jettmar, op. cit., pp. 55-64.
11. Abdul Sattar Khan, "AJK, Fata, GB, capital population goes up many a time", *The News*, April 8, 2012.
12. Ibid.
13. Muhammad Asif Wazir and Anne Goujon, "Assessing the 2017 Census of Pakistan using Demographic Analysis: A Sub-national Perspective", Vienna Institute of Demography Working Papers 06/2019, Vienna: Vienna Institute of Demography, Austrian Academy of Sciences, 2019, p. 5.
14. Pearce Gervis, *This is Kashmir*, London: Cassell & Company Ltd, 1954, pp. 224-227.
15. Maulvi Hashmatullah Khan, *History of Baltistan*, Baltistan Research Translation, Islamabad, Lok Virsa, 1987, pp. 133-134.
16. Shafqat Inqalabi, "Economic Exploitation of Gilgit-Baltistan" in Virendra Gupta and Alok Bansal (ed), *Pakistan Occupied Kashmir: The Untold Story*, New Delhi: Manas Publications, 2007, p. 189.
17. "Pakistan's first Gem Bazaar opens its door to gem-lovers", *Pakistan Observer*, December 24, 2017.
18. Jettmar, op. cit., pp. 41-44.
19. Khan, op. cit., pp. 132-135.
20. Syed Abdul Quddus, *The North-West Frontier of Pakistan*, Karachi: Royal Book Company, 1990, pp. 242-243.
21. Farman Ali, "Gilgit-Baltistan residents request border crossings at Skardu", *The Herald*, April 2005, p. 50.
22. Ershad Mahmud, "Challenges Before the New Government in NAs", *The News*, Internet Edition, December 11, 2004.
23. Aabha Dixit, "Ethnicity and Human Rights" in Jasjit Singh (ed.), *Pakistan Occupied Kashmir: Under the Jackboot*, New Delhi: Siddhi Books, 1995, pp. 197-198.
24. Bansal, op. cit., pp. 80-89.
25. Ibid, pp. 85-90.
26. Ibid, pp. 100-101.

27 Ibid, p. 103.
28 Senge H Sering, "Political Dynamics of Culture and Identity in Baltistan" in K Warikoo (ed.), *The Other Kashmir: Society, Culture and Politics in the Karakoram Himalayas*, New Delhi: Pentagon Press, 2014, pp. 73-74.
29 Alok Bansal, "Sectarian Violence in Gilgit-Baltistan" in Mohammad Monir Alam (ed.), *Pakistan Occupied Kashmir: Internal Dynamics and Externalities*, New Delhi: Academic Publications, 2015, pp. 58-59.
30 Khyber Pakhtunkhwa was then called North West Frontier Province (NWFP).
31 Akbar Hussain Akbar, "Northern Areas (1986-2000)" in Ahmad Hassan Dani (ed.), *History of Northern Areas of Pakistan (Upto 2000 AD)*. Lahore: Sang-e-Meel Publications, 2007, p. 430.
32 Samuel Baid, "Northern Areas" in Jasjit Singh (ed.), *Pakistan Occupied Kashmir: Under the Jackboot*, New Delhi: Siddhi Books, 1995, p. 139.
33 For a detailed analysis of the Shia objections, see Nosheen Ali, Delusional States: Feeling Rule and Development in Pakistan's Northern Frontier, Cambridge: Cambridge University Press, 2019, pp. 126-132.
34 Bansal, "Sectarian Violence in Gilgit-Baltistan", op. cit., pp. 60-62.
35 Bansal, *Gilgit-Baltistan and its Saga*, op. cit., pp. 119-127.
36 Ibid, pp. 97-117.
37 From http://www.jammukashmirnow.com/pok/facts-about-gb (accessed on 14 September 2019).
38 Fahad Shah, "Does the China-Pakistan economic corridor worry India?" Al Jazeera Website; https://www.aljazeera.com/indepth/features/2017/02/china-pakistan-economic-corridor-worry-india-170208063418124.html (accessed on 14 September 2019).
39 Vikram Sood, "Why India cannot afford to give up Siachen", Rediff.Com, April 12, 2012; https://www.rediff.com/news/column/why-india-cannot-afford-to-give-up-siachen/20120413.htm (accessed on 10 January 2020).
40 M Ismail Khan, "Skardu Dam; Recipe for Disaster", *The International News*, Internet Edition, March 16, 2005.
41 Zahid Hameed, "APC slams govt for not consulting NAs residents on building Basha", *Daily Times*, February 16, 2006.
42 Priyanka Singh, "China-Pakistan Water Axis on the Indus", IDSA Issue Brief, July 19, 2017, Institute for Defence Studies and Analyses Website; https://idsa.in/issuebrief/china-pakistan-water-axis-on-the-indus_psingh_190717 (accessed on 15 January 2020).
43 "NA's students claim Chitral as part of Gilgit-Baltistan'; http://www.chitralnews.com/LN144.htm (accessed on 2 March 2006).

6

Chinese Occupied Territory of Ladakh (COTL)

This chapter deals with the regions of the Union Territory of Ladakh under Chinese occupation. There are some significant differences between the territories under Chinese control and those under the Pakistani control, covered in previous two chapters. Unlike POJK and POTL, the region under Chinese occupation, which includes the Trans-Karakoram Shaksgam Valley, unilaterally ceded by Pakistan to China in 1963 as part of a boundary settlement, and Aksai Chin and Western Ladakh, militarily occupied by China in 1962,[1] is more or less totally devoid of any habitation and as such would need to be analysed differently. It would be infructuous to delve over its administration and the treatment of its people as there are virtually none. Moreover, China, unlike Pakistan, does not claim entire Jammu and Kashmir or Ladakh, but only a part of it and its dispute with India is a border dispute, not a territorial one. More significantly, unlike, the Line of Control (LoC) between India and Pakistan, the Line of Actual Control (LAC) between Indian and Chinese positions in Ladakh has neither been delineated on map, nor demarcated on ground. Consequently, the estimation of territory under Chinese control varies based on the alignment of LAC. More significantly, there are territories under Chinese control that should historically be a part of India, but have not been claimed by India since 1947.

To understand the strategic importance of the Chinese Occupied territories of Ladakh (COTL), one has to go back in history and understand the location of Ladakh, which has been at the crossroads of many trade routes. Its proximity to Silk Route and its contiguity with Xinjiang, Central Asia and Tibet made it a significant destination on the trade routes. The main trading centre in Central Asia was Yarkand and the trade route from Yarkand, via Karakoram Pass to Leh and then to Srinagar, was the most popular route. In fact traders from Yarkand and traders from Kashmir and beyond met at the centre point of Leh in Ladakh. The Srinagar-Leh-Yarkand route was the most popular, well maintained and so safe that traders could leave their goods in the case of emergency and move on to the next stage. There were local trade routes from Skardu to Leh to extend the central Asian trade into interiors. [2]

There were winter and summer routes. The winter route was from Digar La, crisscrossing the frozen Shyok river, passing the Karakoram pass, and then descending towards

Yarkand through Karghalik and Kugiar. The summer route from Leh to Yarkand passed through Khardung La, Nubra valley, Saser La, Karakoram Pass and the Suget Pass. Another popular route was cutting through Aksai Chin to join the Leh-Yarkand Route at Shahidullah. This route was developed after a treaty between the Kashmir king and British Government and the highway was tax free for travellers from British India. In 1949, following occupation of Xinjiang, the Nubra valley route was closed. Following occupation of Aksai Chin, the trade route to Yarkand via Shahidullah was also closed.[3]

Leh had a flourishing trade with Tibet through the Leh-Gartok-Lhasa route. Another route went through Demchok. The treaty of Tingmosgang placed at Appendix D, had secured exclusive rights for the lucrative pashmina wool trade to Ladakh. The wool trade was so lucrative that after Ladakh war, the British tried to get exclusive rights over it, leading Zorawar Singh to reclaim the trade by engaging in a war with Tibet leading to the Chushul treaty of 1842, placed at Appendix E, and a subsequent treaty in 1847 to reclaim the wool trade. The pashmina wool trade maintained shawl industries in Kashmir. Travellers have recorded chests full of gold and silver dust that were used for trading. During the Dogra rule, this trade amounted to several lakh rupees. This trade came to a stop after China occupied Tibet and after the Aksai Chin Highway 219 was completed. By 1959, the trade between Tibet and Ladakh came to a virtual standstill.[4]

It is very important to understand the importance of

Ladakh as a thriving trade centre and thus efforts must be made to reopen the Demchok-Minsar route that was closed after 1954 India-China Trade and Transit Treaty. The strategic importance of territories occupied by China in Ladakh can be appreciated better once the trade routes and their context to Ladakh are understood.[5] "Ladakh's geographical position leaves no room for doubt that its ancient caravan routes must have often served as a path first for conquest and then for retreat of the opposing armies as they alternated between victory and defeat".[6]

The territory of Ladakh that has been under Chinese occupation comprises those territories that were directly controlled by Maharaja of Jammu and Kashmir in 1947, or paid taxes to him or his vassal Mir of Hunza. These include Aksai Chin, Trans-Karakoram Tracts, which comprise Shaksgam Valley, Raskam or Yarkand River Valley and Taghdumbash Pamir, and Principality of Minsar. There is an all-pervasive ignorance about all these regions in Indian consciousness. Unlike the territory under Pakistan's occupation, it is not feasible to specify the exact area that is under Chinese control, as the LoC has not been exactly demarcated. As the region, with the exception of Minsar and some villages in Taghdumbash Pamir, is virtually uninhabited, there are no developments that draw media attention apart from 'military incursions' in Aksai Chin.

AKSAI CHIN

The most significant part of the territory under Chinese control is Aksai Chin, an extremely inhospitable and desolate terrain. Most Indians mistakenly consider it to be the only part of India under Chinese occupation. This section will deal with its geography, history, dispute with China, present status and Indian claims.

Geography and History

The area of this extremely inhospitable region is around 37,244 km^2. The region is separated from Tarim Basin in Xinjiang by Kunlun Mountain ranges. The elevation of this high-altitude desert varies from 4300 m at the bed of Karakash River to 7000 m. The western part of Aksai Chin region is drained by the Tarim River. The region as a whole receives little precipitation as the Himalayas and Karakoram block the rains from the Indian monsoon. Karakash River, which originates at an altitude of over 5800 m, northeast of Galwan Kangri peak in the Aksai Chin region, is the most significant river originating in the region. It flows northwards and then westwards to cross Indian borders South of Xaidullah. After 740 km, the river joins Yurungkash River, which also originates in Aksai Chin; the combined river is known as Hotan River, which flows into Tarim River. Karakash and Yurungkash Rivers are also known as Black Jade and White Jade Rivers as they carry jade boulders. Karakash riverbed is the only part of this region where some vegetation appears periodically. Another river that originates in the region is Chip Chap

River, which flows westwards to join Shyok River in Ladakh. The eastern part of the region contains several small endorheic basins and contains many soda and salt water lakes. The largest salt water lake is Aksai Chin Lake, which is fed by a river of the same name. Other saltwater lakes in the region are Surigh yil ganning kol, Tso tang and Hongshan hu. Much of the northern part of Aksai Chin is referred to as the Soda Plains.[7] The region is covered with soda and has frequent soda dust storms, which make habitation even more difficult.[8]

Historically, the region was the eastern part of Ladakh, located in the north-western part of the Tibetan plateau and south of Kunlun Mountains. It was not part of any ancient empire, as owing to its elevation it was considered unsuitable for habitation. However, in due course the region became a transit zone for traders and hosted two flourishing trade routes connecting Lhasa (in Tibet), Leh (in India) and Kashgar (in China), through which caravans of Yaks passed through in summer months. Historically, armies tend to tread the routes taken by trade caravans, and consequently, the region was also transited by various armies moving to/from Xinjiang or Tibet. The growing significance of the region, due to its trade routes led to contestation between Tibet and Ladakh over this crucial region. After numerous conflicts between the two, Treaty of Tingmosgang was signed, which delineated the border between the two states and placed this region within the territory of Ladakh. However, despite being part of the territory of Ladakh's ruler, no attempt was made to occupy it, considering the hostile terrain and climatic conditions. Consequently, the Dzungar Khanate used it to attack Tibet in 1717, as this was the only route from Tarim Basin to Tibet that was passable all year round.[9]

As Ladakh came under the sway of Maharaja Gulab Singh, he inherited its boundaries with Tibet. In 1842, in a treaty signed between Gulab Singh and Tibetans, both agreed to stick to old agreed boundaries.[10] The area was uninhibited except for caravans passing through, and nomads coming for grazing and to collect Salt. There were two historic trade routes crisscrossing Aksai Chin that ended at Shahidulla (Xaidulla), which was a frontier post of the kingdom of Jammu and Kashmir till 1866. One was along the western limits and the other along the eastern boundary of Chang Chenmo valley.[11] Ever since the establishment of the kingdom of Jammu and Kashmir, the areas up to the frontiers were regularly administered and the check posts on the trade routes were marked on the maps from 1865 onwards.[12]

Understanding the Aksai Chin Dispute

After the East India Company defeated the Sikh empire, by Treaty of Amritsar in 1846, the British recognised Gulab Singh, as Maharaja of Jammu and Kashmir. Since Gulab Singh had already accepted British paramountcy, the border between Kashmir and Tibet became a matter of negotiation between the British and the Chinese. Within three months of the Treaty of Amritsar, British constituted a commission to delineate the Eastern boundaries of Jammu and Kashmir with Tibet. The British had accordingly asked Maharaja to depute two intelligent officers to work with the officers of the boundary commission. The two boundary commissions of 1846 and 1847 failed to get the cooperation of Chinese officials. The commission clearly placed Chang Chenmo valley well within Ladakh and Lanak La at the eastern extremity as part of Kashmir.[13]

The survey work in Kashmir to determine India's boundary began in 1855, and WH Johnson, a civilian sub-assistant to Major Montgomery, was assigned the task to survey the North Eastern Ladakh. He remained in Ladakh in 1865, at a time when the Chinese rule over Xinjiang had totally collapsed and a new state of Kashgaria had emerged. However, by 1877, China had reconquered Kashgaria, which was afflicted by frequent internecine wars. Initially after the conquest of Kashgar, Chinese treated Kunlun Mountains as their Southern boundary, but subsequently, moved further southward. In 1890, Captain Younghusband, who had gone to Pamirs, was told that Karakoram Mountains constituted China's Southern boundary. To further assert their claim, Chinese unilaterally established boundary markers at Karakoram Pass in 1892; however, it was not objected to by the British. Keith Johnston's Atlas of 1894 clearly showed Aksai Chin within India. This showed the boundary of Ladakh as running along Kunlun Mountains to a point East of 80° East and was similar to Johnson's position. However, in 1896, there were some protests from Chinese authorities on the depiction of Aksai Chin as part of Kashmir.[14]

The White Paper of the Ministry of External Affairs documents the revenue collection by the Maharaja's administration:

> The arrangements made by the Governments of India and Kashmir for the establishment and maintenance of trade routes across Aksai Chin, the provision of facilities such as rest houses and store houses for those using these routes and the regular use of these routes as of right by Indian trading parties - both official and unofficial - constituted powerful evidence of Indian administrative jurisdiction in the 19th century up to the traditional boundary claimed by India. The very fact that there were never any disputes about the exercise of such jurisdiction and the use of these routes by Indians as of right showed that there could have been no difference of opinion in those times between the Ladakhis on the one hand and the authorities of Sinkiang and Tibet on the other as to where the boundary lay.

> In 1866, on receipt of complaints that trade with Yarkand was suffering due to excessive duties levied by the Kashmir Government, the Government of India entered into negotiations with the Government of Kashmir for developing a new route from Chushul along the Pangong lake and across Lingzi Tang and Aksai Chin to Shahidulla, and creating other facilities. In May 1870, the two parties signed an agreement. Article 1 of this treaty stated,

> With the consent of the Maharaja, officers of the British Government will be appointed to survey the trade routes through the Maharaja's territories from the British frontier of Lahoul to the territories of the Ruler of Yarkhand, including the route via the Chang Chemoo Valley. The Maharaja will depute an officer of his

Government to accompany the surveyors, and will render them all the assistance in his power. A map of the routes surveyed will be made an attested copy of which will be given to the Maharaja.[15]

Further revenue records and maps prove that the area was administered by the Maharaja of Jammu and Kashmir:

> Mangal Mehta, wazir of Ladakh during 1860-65, organized the revenue settlement of the whole area. In the regular revenue assessment reports the names of areas and villages and the amount of revenue collected from each of them, which is now claimed by China as having been under their administrative jurisdiction for centuries, were included. The report of 1908 mentioned 108 villages including Tankse, Demchok and Minsar and mentions Aksai Chin, Lingzi Tang where rights of pastures and salt collection were exercised, as parts of Tankse ilaqa. The preliminary report of Ladakh settlement outlined a revenue and political history of these areas. The boundary question found direct and indirect mention in these reports. The assessment report of Ladakh tehsil of 1909 stated, "There have been no boundary disputes on the Lhasa frontiers and the existing boundary seems to be well understood by the subjects of both the state and the Lhasa Government".[16]

The India-China border problem has a colonial legacy. The British drew different lines to denote the limits of the empire on various maps at different times, depending on their perception and suitability. The boundaries were never demarcated physically and remained only on the map. The three boundary lines were Johnson Line (1865), Johnson-Ardagh Line (1897), and Macartney-MacDonald Line (1899).[17]

Johnson Line

As brought out earlier, William Johnson, a civil servant with the Survey of India, proposed the "Johnson Line" in 1865, which put Aksai Chin in Kashmir. This was the time of the Dungan revolt when China did not control most of Xinjiang, so this Line was never presented to the Chinese. Johnson presented this Line to the Maharaja Ranbir Singh of Jammu and Kashmir, who then claimed the territory further north as far as Sanju Pass in the Kunlun Mountains. He had already established a fort at Shahidulla and positioned his troops there in 1863, thereby bringing Yarkand River valley between the Karakoram and Kunlun ranges under his control. However, extremely inhospitable conditions forced Maharaja's troops to vacate Shahidulla in 1866.[18] The boundary of Ladakh according to Johnson Line (boundary drawn by Johnson on map) included all the territory between Karkoram Pass and Kunlun mountains. The first edition of Survey of India maps of Turkestan also clearly followed Johnson Line.[19] There is clear evidence to indicate that even besides the troops, civilian custom officials of Maharaja were present at Shahidulla till November 1866.[20] Even in 1889, when Russian explorer Captain Grombtchevsky visited Shahidulla, he expected it to be occupied by Kashmiri troops. He was, however, informed that Kashmiri troops had withdrawn because Chinese had prohibited export of provisions from Sanju and Kilian. After their withdrawal, Chinese came to Shahidulla and arrested 'Beg' appointed by Chinese and replaced him with a new Beg and left.[21]

Johnson-Ardagh Line

In 1897, a British military officer, Sir John Ardagh, proposed a boundary line along the crest of the Kunlun Mountains north of the Yarkand River.[22] At the time, Britain was concerned at the prospects of Russian expansion as China weakened; Ardagh argued that this line was more defensible. The Ardagh Line was really a modification of the Johnson Line, and became known as the "Johnson-Ardagh Line".[23]

Macartney-MacDonald Line

In 1893, Hung Ta-chen, a senior Chinese official at St. Petersburg, gave maps of the region to George Macartney, British consul general at Kashgar, which coincided in broad details with the Johnson Line. In 1899, London proposed a revised boundary, initially suggested by Macartney and developed by the Governor General of India, Lord Elgin. This boundary placed the Lingzi Tang plains, which are south of the Laktsang range in India, and Aksai Chin proper, which is north of the Laktsang range, in China. This border, along the Karakoram Mountains, was proposed and supported by British officials primarily to create a Chinese buffer to prevent Russia's advance in Central Asia. Macartney-MacDonald Line was presented to the Chinese in Peking (Beijing) by Sir Claude MacDonald on 24 March 1899 in a note. The Qing government did not respond to the note, and the British took that as Chinese acquiescence. Although no official boundary had ever been negotiated, China claimed that this had been the accepted boundary since 1949 when the People's Republic of China was established.[24]

The Johnson-Ardagh and Macartney-MacDonald Lines were both used on British maps of India. Until at least 1908, the British took the MacDonald Line as the boundary, but in 1911, the Xinhai Revolution resulted in the collapse of central power in China and by the end of World War I, the British officially used the Johnson Line. In 1912, it was the British Foreign Secretary McMahon himself who demanded that India should maintain Johnson-Ardagh Line as the boundary.[25] From 1917 to 1933, the Postal Atlas of China, published by the Government of China in Peking, depicted the boundary in Aksai Chin as per the Johnson Line, which runs along the Kunlun Mountains.[26] The Peking University Atlas, published in 1925, also put Aksai Chin in India.[27] When British officials learned that Soviet officials were surveying Aksai Chin for Sheng Shicai, the warlord of Xinjiang in 1940-1941, they again advocated the Johnson Line.[28] None of these boundaries were ever demarcated on ground; they existed only on maps according to the prevailing British Interests.

Indian Independence and Chinese Occupation

At independence, the Government of India used the Johnson-Ardagh Line as the basis for its official boundary in the west, which included Aksai Chin. From the Karakoram Pass (which is not under dispute), the Indian claim line extends northeast of the Karakoram Mountains through the salt flats of Aksai Chin to set a boundary at the Kunlun Mountains, and incorporating part of the Karakash and Yarkand River watersheds. From there, it runs east along the Kunlun Mountains before turning southwest through

CHINESE OCCUPIED TERRITORY OF LADAKH (COTL)

the Aksai Chin salt flats, through the Karakoram range, and then to Pangong Lake.[29] On 1 July 1954, Prime Minister Jawaharlal Nehru wrote a memo directing revision of maps of India to show definite boundaries on all frontiers. Hitherto, the boundary in Aksai Chin sector, based on the Johnson Line, had been described as "undemarcated".[30]

China occupied this region by building China Highway 219 linking Lazi in the Tibet autonomous region to Xinjiang between 1951 and 1957. On 6 October 1957, a Chinese newspaper, *Kuang-Ming Jih Pao*, reported, "The Sinkiang-Tibet—the highest highway in the world—has been completed". The region had a flourishing trade in 1953, with Tibetan traders carrying tea, incense and veils for sale in Leh, returning with soap, cigarettes, sugar and dried fruits, while traders from Leh carried wheat, flour, barley and eggs to Tibet and returned with wool and silver coins. The trade route ran from Khotan (Hotan) to Sugat Karaul and Shahidulla Mazar and then to Kargilik and Kashgar, while another route passed through Karakoram Pass and the Depsang plain. This is clearly a very strategic territory. Trade ended with the construction of the Aksai Chin highway.[31]

After the occupation of Tibet by China, India tried to maintain friendly relations with China and entered into an India-China Trade and Transit Treaty incorporating Panchsheel on 28 April 1954, after surrendering existing ancient rights in Tibet. India assumed that China had accepted the existing traditional boundary along the Indo-Tibet border, but were rudely disillusioned when China released maps showing most of Ladakh and North East region under it. On 4 September 1958, when the Aksai Chin Highway had been made Public, PM Nehru stated, "So far as the Broad boundary, the international frontier between India and China state, including the Tibetan region is concerned, it is not a matter of dispute as far as we are concerned, it is a fixed thing". He accordingly instructed the foreign secretary to lodge an informal protest with the Chinese Embassy. On 18 October 1958, the Indian foreign secretary handed over an 'informal note' to the Chinese ambassador in New Delhi.[32]

Correspondence between Indian and Chinese PM followed. On 23 January 1959, the Chinese PM stated that the India-China borders had never been delimited. Three rounds of India-China Boundary Talks followed in 1959-1960, where India put forward more than 650 items to buttress its claim on Aksai Chin. The events came to a head when Dalai Lama fled to India along with thousands of Tibetans. Public opinion in India grew against China and supported Tibetans. On 8 September 1959, Chinese PM made it very clear that it claimed large swaths of Indian territory in Ladakh and North East as its own. Nehru laid all the India-China correspondence in the Parliament and the contents created a public opinion against China. Nehru had talks with Zhou en Lai from 19 to 25 April 1960, which were a diplomatic failure. On 2 November 1961, Nehru issued a Forward Policy for the Indian Army wherein forward posts were to be maintained and patrols carried out to prevent further ingress by the Chinese. On 30 April 1962, China termed forward patrols as incursions and

CHINESE OCCUPIED TERRITORY OF LADAKH (COTL)

threatened to start Chinese patrols in the Karakoram pass region. On 26 May 1962, China announced Trans-Karakoram boundary talks with Pakistan; this territory included the Pakistan-occupied territory of Gilgit-Baltistan. After months of diplomatic exchanges on 'incursions' on 20 October 1962, China invaded India across the entire boundary in a synchronised event. After nearly a month of fighting, on 21 November 1962, China announced a unilateral ceasefire, occupying Aksai Chin since then.[33]

Present Status

Today most of the Aksai Chin is under Chinese occupation. Most of it is administered as part of Hotan County, which lies in the South-eastern part of Hotan Prefecture of Xinjiang Autonomous Region. Some part in South including Demchok and a small territory in extreme East is administratively part of Tibetan Autonomous Region.

The region is largely uninhabited with the exception of the divided village of Demchok,[34] where Chinese have built some modern buildings to woo citizens of border villages. In addition, PLA has built two military stations on Highway 219 (Aksai Chin Road) in Tianshuihai village at an elevation of 4890 m and Tielongtan. At both the places, some hotels and gas stations have come up and they act as transit halts for people travelling along the highway. Nomadic tribes still go grazing in the region; however, the movement of graziers from the Indian part has over the years stopped as Indian security forces do not allow them to cross their perceived LAC.

TRANS-KARAKORAM TRACTS

Of Trans-Karakoram tracts, Raskam Valley and Taghdumbash Pamir were the regions from where revenue was collected by the Mir of Hunza (the ruler of Hunza) and which were consequently included within the boundaries of Jammu and Kashmir as per Johnson Line. Taghdumbash lies to the north of the Hindu Kush and was connected to Hunza through Kilik and Mintaka passes.[35] However, the status of Hunza was a complex one as it paid tribute both to Jammu and Kashmir, as well as the Chinese Emperor. In March 1899, the British through a note from Sir Claude Maxwell MacDonald, who was the British Minister to the Empire of China based in Peking (Beijing), formally proposed that China relinquishes suzerainty over Hunza, and Hunza in turn gives up most of the Taghdumbash Pamir and Raskam Valley. However, there was no Chinese response. Meanwhile, the boundary presented by Sir MacDonald in his 14 March 1899 dispatch had included a red line in frontier which included upper portion of the Taghdumbash, westward of Mintaka Aksai and the darwaza post on far side of Shimshal pass. However, nomadic tribes continued to move their cattle flocks for grazing within the region and kept paying tribute to the Mir of Hunza till 1937. The only significant settlement in the region was the village of Dafdar, inhabited primarily by Wakhis at an altitude of 3400 m in the heart of the Taghdumbash Pamir.[36] It is currently part of Tashkurgan Tajik Autonomous County in Kashgar Prefecture of Xinjiang. The exact circumstances under which the people from this region stopped paying tribute to Hunza are not quite clear.

From 1899 till 1947, when India attained independence, depiction of border on various maps varied. In 1926, renowned British geographer Kenneth Mason surveyed Shaksgam Valley, which was South of MacDonald Line. Apparently, British Indian Government relinquished claims to areas north of MacDonald Line in this sector in 1927, although this is not reflected in the maps published in that period. Although the Government of India now does not claim Raskam Valley or Taghdumbash, it is not clear as to when this position was arrived at, because Jawaharlal Nehru in a telegram to British PM Clement Attlee on 26 October 1947 stated, "Jammu and Kashmir's Northern frontiers, as you are aware, run in common with those of three countries, Afghanistan, the Union of Soviet Socialist Republics and China".[37] This implies that he considered Taghdumbash to be a part of Jammu and Kashmir.

After the 1962 Sino-Indian conflict, the convergence of Chinese and Pakistani positions resulted in Pakistan handing over Shaksgam Valley to China. On 2 March 1963, Zulfiqar Ali Bhutto and Cheng Li signed a provisional agreement in Beijing to allow China to occupy Shaksgam, Raskam, Shimshal and Aghil valleys of Gilgit-Baltistan.[38] China gained approximately 5309 km^2 of territory in Shaksgam Valley, while it relinquished its claims over Hunza. The agreement was primarily an outcome of the Sino-Indian conflict. The actual demarcation work was eventually completed in March 1965.[39] The brief description along with a history of three Trans-Karakoram territories is given in succeeding pages.

SHAKSGAM VALLEY

Shaksgam Valley is the valley around Shaksgam River, a left tributary of Yarkand River, which originates from the glaciers in Karakoram and flows northwest parallel to the Karakoram ridge. Historically, the bed of the Yarkand River where Shaksgam joins it was used for cultivation by farmers from the state of Hunza. The rest of the area is used as pastures by yak herdsmen from Hunza. The rulers of Hunza had traditional rights over this territory. An extremely inhospitable terrain, Shaksgam Valley had no permanent habitation. Historically, a large number of traders and pilgrims travelling from China, Russia, Central Asian republics to India, Afghanistan and Persia and beyond would traverse through the region.

During colonial times, the region was acknowledged as the part of the State of Hunza, and being on the main trade route, it was surveyed by the British. Grassy valleys were ideal for grazing and Kyrgyz nomads regularly came here with their herds and paid taxes to the Mir of Hunza. The rulers of Hunza treated collecting tax from the caravans as their right and paid tribute to China along with the Kashmir Durbar. Captain Younghusband states in a secret note that the nomads like Kyrgyz did not consider any frontiers and travelled across boundaries without fear.[40]

The Trans-Karakoram tracts were ruled by the Mir of Hunza, who was a vassal of the king of Jammu and Kashmir and paid tribute to the Maharaja of J&K ever since Anglo-Brusho War fought from 1 to 23 December 1891 between the troops of the British Raj and Nagar and Hunza states. After the accession of J&K to the Dominion of India, Hunza also became a part of India. However, after the occupation of Gilgit-Baltistan by Pakistan, the Mir of Hunza signed an accession letter with Pakistan. This accession was illegal as the Mir, being a vassal of Maharaja Hari Singh, had no authority to sign an accession letter. In 1963, Pakistan, without approval of the Mir of Hunza, ceded Shaksgam Valley to China.

The official Indian and Chinese maps such as that of Hung Ta Chen and Postal Atlases of China of 1917, 1919 and 1993 showed Indian administrative control up to the alignment west of Karakoram pass. The Mir of Hunza too had for centuries exerted sovereign control over south of Mustagh and Aghil Range.[41] Shaksgam Valley has cultural links with Baltistan. The language spoken is Balti. The names of the places in Shaksgam are in Balti. Famous camping grounds of Moni Brangsa (residence of Musicians), Balti Brangsa (Balti residence) and Balti Pulo (dwellings of the Baltis) prove links of Shaksgam with Baltistan. The Raja of Shigar had laid out a polo ground called Muztaghi Shagaran in the south of Shaksgam Valley in the 5th century AD.

Pakistan agreed in May 1962 to negotiate with China regarding part of the border of Kashmir with Sinkiang. As Pakistan has no border with China, the Government of India protested to both China and Pakistan over the illegality of their negotiations, reaffirmed India's sovereignty over the territory concerned and declared that

India would not recognise any demarcation of the borders by them. However, on 26 and 28 December 1962, it was announced that China and Pakistan had agreed in principle on the location and alignment of the boundary actually existing between the two countries and intended to sign a border agreement on this basis. The Indian delegation, then at Rawalpindi, protested that neither of the nations had any locus standi in the region.

On 2 March 1963, Pakistan further violated the UNCIP resolution as well as the UN Security Council resolutions, when it entered into an agreement with China and altered the position in J&K by transferring close to 1,868 square miles of the northern territory to China. Nevertheless, Pakistan, in the Sino-Pakistan Border Agreement of 1963, accepted once again that the sovereignty of the region did not rest with it, as Article 6 of the document read: The two parties have agreed that after the settlement of the Kashmir dispute between Pakistan and India, the sovereign authority concerned will reopen negotiations with the Government of the People's Republic of China on the boundary as described in Article Two of the present agreement, so as to sign a formal boundary treaty to replace the present agreement, provided that in the event of the sovereign authority being Pakistan, the provisions of the present agreement and of the aforesaid protocol shall be maintained in the formal boundary treaty to be signed between the People's Republic of China and Pakistan. Prime Minister Nehru, on 5 March 1963, informed the Parliament that Pakistan had ceded over 5000 km^2 of Indian territory to China.[42]

Present State of Shaksgam

Shaksgam Valley is a very important land link between China and Pakistan and is a very important part of China-Pakistan Economic Corridor (CPEC). China has built many feeder roads in Shaksgam, connecting Gilgit with Hotan, a military headquarter at the cross section of Tibet-Xinjiang highway and Hotan-Golmund Highway. This highway cuts the distance of Gilgit to Golmund by nearly half. Another feeder road has been built across the southern rim of Xinjiang connecting Gilgit with Aksai Chin.

RASKAM VALLEY

Raskam Valley or Yarkand Valley is the upper valley of Yarkand River, where it is called Raskam. It lay on the trade routes and Mir of Hunza collected tax from the caravans passing through it and shared them with Maharaja and China. Like Shaksgam, Raskam was also surveyed by the Britishers. The rulers of Hunza also carried raids across the Raskam area and were active participants in the slave trade carried by Kyrghyz. Subsequently, when Raskam was under Chinese and Russian control, people from Hunza were given tracts to do agriculture during summers. In late 1880s, the Pamirs became a chessboard for greater games with China, Russia and Britain becoming stakeholders. In 1904, secret declassified documents by MEA show that Hunza collected taxes from Raskam. Fearing Chinese invasion, or Russians supplanting China, the British were planning to ask Mir of Hunza to end his relation with China, while respecting his rights to collect taxes in Taghdumbash Pamir and Raskam. The boundary drawn in 1899 contained the Area of Northern Taghdumbash and Darwaza, and in a secret note of 2 November 1904, Captain Younghusband suggested, "Send a notification to Chinese, that, since they have been unable to fulfil their promises to Mir of Hunza, That state, under advise of British Government, withdraws from all relations with China". There was no cessation of rights of Mir of Hunza at this point; the rights would be withdrawn for concessions, if need arose. However, there is no proof that they were ever withdrawn.[43]

On Raskam and Shaksgam, the following observations

can be found: "On some maps the northern boundary of Kashmir Territory and the Eastern boundary of Mir's territory is shown along the Gasherbrum, K2, the Mustagh Pass, and the northwards by the eastern watershed of the Ghujereb-Khunjereb basin.... Prior to the eighties in the last century the areas called Raskam were Grazed by the Khirgiz ... it is equally certain that any authority carried weight in those days was the authority of Mir of Hunza ... when the Khirgiz here thought it was time to make objection, they appealed to China, and were told they lived beyond the authority of Chinese. They appealed to India, ... Captain Younghusband was sent to enquire, Sir Francis found Hunza posts established down Shingahal valley down beyond Shingahal pass...."[44]

It must be noted that Captain Younghusband named the valley upstream of Shingahal valley Shaksgam, which was wrongly called Oprang, and had dismissed any claim of Chinese on Shaksgam Valley.[45]

Secret papers accessed show that the British were very eager that the Mir of Hunza gave up any relation with China. The Mir paid an annual tribute to the Emperor of China in Kashghar. In return, the Mir was allowed to collect taxes in Taghdumbash and in Raskam. The Mir of Hunza was allotted 5 tracts in Raskam for carrying out farming in summers. By 1900s, there was Russian presence in Raskam along with Chinese, and the Hunzas were "ousted" from Raskam. However, the Officials in Kashgar assured the Mir of Hunza that his rights in Raskam were ancient and would be respected. The British advised the Mir of Hunza to take this opportunity to sever all relations with China. The British offered to compensate the Mir with Rs. 3000 per annum towards the loss he would incur by not collecting tribute in Raskam and the annual Chinese presents he received (valued at Rs. 1600). Further, the British proposed to settle the excess Hunza men in Gilgit area and employ about 250 men as Levy.

Claims of Hunza in Raskam

The claims of Hunza over Raskam are substantiated by various records in the Foreign Office. According to declassified secret files, by July 1898, the Britishers were informed that the Chinese in Yarkand had assured the Mir of Hunza that their rights in Raskam will be protected and they would be given 6 tracts for farming. A letter from Taotai of Kashgar to the Mir of Hunza dated 27 April 1898 assuring that the lands in Raskam will be given to Hunza is proof of Hunza claims in Raskam. However, there was no further action. On 8 March 1904, another letter from the Taotai of Kashgar to the Mir of Hunza was recorded, which detailed the tribute paid by Hunza and the presents given by Chinese.

By 1904, the British had suggested that the Chinese be informed that as China could not protect Mir of Hunza's rights in Raskam, the Mir, under the advice of British Consul, was withdrawing from all relations with Chinese. By March 1905, the same had been communicated to China. It must be understood that after annexation of Hunza by British, the traditional rights of Hunza underwent a change in the Trans-Karakoram area. The British recorded the same by recognising that post annexation of Hunza, the raids of Hunza in Trans-Karakoram tracts had lessened and the authority had diminished. In 1904-1905, the Mir of Hunza gave up claims in Raskam and cut off all relations with China, under the advice of the British. [46]

TAGHDUMBASH PAMIR

Tagdumbash Pamir is a high valley to the west of Karakoram, currently part of Tashkurgan Tajik Autonomous County, in Xinjiang, China. However, a perusal of secret declassified documents of British India makes it clear that Taghdumbash Pamirs were treated as a part of the northern boundary of Kashmir state. In 1930, while drawing new Maps of India, the following observations were made: "The Russian claims on the Pamirs ... ends at the watershed on the Taghdumbash...." "In 1913, the Mir of Hunza had his yaks grazing in the Taghdumbash ... and he told us the head of this was his" "To my mind the whole of the two basins of Khunjereb and Gunjerab belong to the Mir".[47]

The information regarding Taghdumbash is sketchy and gleaned mostly from various travel books written by explorers or British Officers who were sent to survey and explore the Pamirs. Captain Younghusband explored the Taghdumbash in summer of 1890-91. He reported that Pamirs were reported to be Chinese territory. In 1891, while camping in Taghdumbash, he reported that Russian Military detachment had entered the Pamirs and proclaimed them Russian territory. Many Kyrghyz, inhabitants of little Pamir, had fled to Taghdumbash.[49]

The 1911 Encyclopedia Britannica reports the following about Taghdumbash Pamir, "To the east of the Sarikol chain is the Taghdumbash Pamir, which claims many of the characteristics of the western Pamirs at its upper or western extremity, where the Karachukar, which drains it, is a comparatively small stream. But where the Karachukar, joining forces with the Khunjerab, stretches out northwards for a comparatively straight run to Tashkurghan, dividing asunder the two parallel ranges of Sarikol and Kandar, which together form the Sarikol chain".

The Murtagh chain, which holds within its grasp the mightiest system of glaciers in the world, forms a junction with the Sarikol at the head of the Taghdumbash, where also another great system (that of the Hindu Kush) has its eastern roots. The political boundary between the extreme north of the Kashmir dependencies and the extreme south of Chinese Turkestan is carried by the Zarafshan or Raskam river that runs parallel to the Murtagh at its northern foot (its valley dividing the Murtagh from the Kuen Lun) to a point at about 79°20'E, where it is transferred to the watershed of the Kuen Lun.

The Taghdumbash Pamir occupies a geographical position of some political significance. One important pass (the Beyik, 15,100 ft.) leads from the Russian Pamirs into Sarikol across its northern border. A second pass (the Wakhjir, 16,150 ft) connects the head of the Wakhan valley of Afghanistan Pamir with the Sarikol province across its western head, whilst a third (the Kilik, 15,600 ft) leads into the head of the Hunza river and opens a difficult and dangerous route to Gilgit. The Taghdumbash is claimed both by China and Kanjut (or Hunza), and there is consequently an open boundary question at this corner of the Pamirs.[50]

According to Baroness Emma Nicholson of the UK Conservative Party, "All the evidence points to the fact that

Gilgit and Baltistan region were constituent parts of Jammu and Kashmir by 1877". They remained in this princely domain till the date of accession "in its entirety to the new Dominion of India" on 26 October 1947. This was reiterated in the correspondence of Maharaja Hari Singh (26 October 1947) with Lord Louis Mountbatten, Governor General of India, which states that the state of Jammu and Kashmir has a common boundary with the "Soviet Republic", which *inter alia* alludes to the fact that Gilgit and Kanjut (which includes the Raskam, Hunza Valley and Taghdumbash) are integral parts of Jammu and Kashmir.

The issue of Taghdumbash Pamir needs to be reopened and understood before any closure on Indian claim over the area. Secret papers of British regarding Taghdumbash have firmed up claims of Hunza on Taghdumbash. In 1904, the British wanted proof of Hunza claims on Taghdumbash so that they could use it as concession in a projected severance of relations between Hunza and China. The Kashgar Diaries noted that till 1904, the Mir of Hunza collected taxes from Taghdumbash. Also, he collected tribute from Wakhis who came to the area in summers. A letter from the Amban of Sarikul regarding Taghdumbash tribute was recorded as proof of the Hunza claim.

Taghdumbash Pamir was inhabited by Wakhis, Sarikuls, Kirghiz and Hunza tribes called Kanjuts. These people would inhabit the area in summers, though later reports suggest some settled there for agriculture and built huts and homes.

MINSAR

Minsar, a village located in a broad valley in western Tibet, 32 miles west of Mount Kailash, has been part of the kingdom of Jammu and Kashmir for centuries. The revenue received from it was used to maintain Kailash Mansarovar pilgrimage and had been ceded to the king of Ladakh under a peace treaty signed between Ladakh and Tibet in Tingmosgang in 1684, which stated, "The King of Ladakh reserves to himself the village of Minsar in Ngari-Khorsum (western Tibet)".[51] When Ladakh was incorporated in Maharaja Gulab Singh's kingdom, it became part of Jammu Kashmir State. Maharaja Hari Singh's accession made it an Indian Territory. In 1841-1842, during the War between Kashmir and Tibet, General Zorawar Singh Camped in Minsar. Supply of J&K Army was stored in Minsar. The friendship treaty at Chushul was signed on 17 September 1842.[52] During the time of Mehta Basti Ram, in about 1853, a sum of Rs. 56 was collected from Minsar.

In 1865, WH Johnson, a civil servant with the Survey of India proposed the "Johnson Line", to mark India's borders with China. He talks about Minsar village in Tibet as located beyond Rudok and Gartok at Latitude 31°10' North Longitude 80°50' East. The annual revenue from Minsar was Rs. 500.[53] All subsequent treaties with Tibet retained Minsar as a territory of Kashmir and it continued to be a centre for traders to rest and trade. After accession to India, it is recorded that traders from Uttarakhand and Himachal Pradesh trading in southwest Tibet through old established trading routes visited Minsar and stayed there.

The tour report of Faqir Chand, Wazir Wazarat of Ladakh in 1905, stated that the village of Minsar belonged to Ladakh and that a sum of Rs. 297 was being collected annually as revenue from Minsar. The Assessment Report of 1905, the Final Assessment Report of 1908 and the Settlement Officer's report regarding the amount of revenue payable had all mentioned Minsar. The census reports of 1911 and 1921 also included Minsar. Ladakh Tehsil revenue records show the amount of revenue due as well as the amount actually paid by Minsar for the years 1900-1901, 1901-1902, 1904-1905, 1905-1906, 1908-1909 and 1909-1910. The consolidated register of Ladakh Tehsil contains statements of annual dues and receipts from Minsar village from 1901 to 1937.[54]

In the Census Report of 1921, Minsar was included. Minsar had 44 houses, 87 men and 73 women. In 1929, E.B. Wakefield, an ICS officer, visited western Tibet, and reported that Minsar paid taxes to Kashmir while at the same time fulfilling certain labour obligations to the Tibetan authorities. Every year, the Lumberdar of Rupshu, or some petty official, from Ladakh comes to Minsar to collect the tribute due to the Maharaja of Kashmir. In 1939, 10 years later, Dr Kanshi Ram, the British Trade Agent, visited Minsar. In 1940, Tsetan Phuntsog, a senior Ladakhi official visited Minsar on behalf of the Kashmir government. Abdul Wahid Radhu, a Ladakhi Muslim merchant, passed through Minsar in 1942 as a member of the lo phyag mission to Lhasa, this being the last such mission. Ladakh's triennial lo phyag mission to Lhasa was to carry presents to Lhasa, a product of the 1684 treaty of Tingmosgang.[55]

After independence, in 1950, a special officer, N. Rigzen Ghagil Kalon, was deputed by Jammu and Kashmir State to visit Minsar. His report was forwarded by the Jammu and Kashmir Government to the Ministry of States on September 13, 1950 as 'Note on Conditions of Kashmir Village in Minsar in western Tibet', wherein he reported that the total population of Minsar was 271. The revenue from the village was collected till 1950s. In 1954, Ven. Kushok Bakula Rinpoche, then a Minister in J&K Government visited Manasarovar, along with Sonam Khangsar, a Judicial Clerk of the Leh District Commissioner Office, via Demchok; they collected taxes from the Minsar villagers.[56] Minsar was not discussed during India-China talks from 1954 to 1962, but regrettably remains under Chinese occupation.[57]

Present Position of Minsar

At present, the village is called Men-Shi and is located at the southern end of Gar (Gartok) on national highway 219 in Ngari prefecture. The nearest Indian territories are Malari and Niti Pass in Uttarakhand. For decades, post-1962, Minsar remained a forgotten footnote in the larger boundary issue. However, the people of Ladakh kept the issue alive. In Lok Sabha, since 1982, the MP from Ladakh had raised the question on the situation of Minsar but had got no satisfactory reply. Presently, the issue of Minsar has not been settled legally. The question of enclaves with Bangladesh has been settled with amendment to Article 1. In Minsar's case, neither have the old treaties been revoked, nor has been compensation claimed in lieu of Minsar; the issue hasn't been discussed with China post-1960. Tibet could mange the Bhutani and Ladakhi enclaves without problem for centuries because of the unique relation between Ladakh and Tibet. In modern context, a solution needs to be worked out. A recognition of Indian rights to Minsar and of Indian right to worship at Kailash Mansarovar is of prime importance. Bringing the limelight on Minsar, now a part of UT of Ladakh, becomes more pressing in the light of China celebrating its National Day on 29 September 2019 in Minsar.

NOTES

1. BG Verghese, "A Jammu and Kashmir Primer: From Myth to Reality", Centre for Policy Research, New Delhi, Occasional Paper No. 14, p. 4.
2. K Warikoo, "Ladakh: India's Gateway to Central Asia" in K Warikoo (ed.), *Central Asia and South Asia: Energy Cooperation and Transport Linkages.* New Delhi: Pentagon Press, 2011, pp. 240-241.
3. Ibid, pp. 241-246.
4. Ibid, pp. 242-243. Also see Janet Rizvi, "Trans-Himalayan Caravans: Merchant Princes and Peasant Traders in Ladakh. New Delhi: Oxford University Press, pp. 19-20, 199.
5. Ibid, pp. 246-247.
6. Margaret W Fishcher et al, Himalayan Battleground: Sino-Indian Rivalry in Ladakh, New York: Frederick A Praeger, 1963, pp. 12-15.
7. "Disputed Indian Borders"; https://disputedindia.weebly.com/aksai-chin.html (accessed on 28 December 2018).
8. Hriday Nath Kaul, *India China Boundary in Kashmir,* New Delhi: Gyan Publishing House, 2009, p. 110.
9. Alok Bansal, "Gilgit-Baltistan and Aksai Chin" in Alok Bansal and Aayushi Ketkar (eds), Geopolitics of Himalayan Region: Cultural, Political and Strategic Dimensions, New Delhi, Pentagon Press, 2019, p. 171.
10. Kaul, op. cit., pp. 37-38.
11. The two routes are:

(a) Along the western limits of the Chang Chenmo valley-Shamal Lungpa-Samsung Ling-Dehra Compa-Quila Jilga-Cung Tash-crossing Tag Pass-Chibra valley-Malikshah to Shahidullah.

(b) Along the eastern boundary of Chang Chenmo valley-Nischu-Linzi Tang-Lake Tsund-Thaldut-Khitai Pass-Haji Langar and along Qara Kash (Karakash) valley to Shahidulla.

12   http://chinaindiaborderdispute.wordpress.com/ (accessed on 28 December 2019).
13   Arun Kumar Banerji, "Borders" in Jayanta Kumar Ray (ed.), *Aspects of India's International Relations 1700 to 2000: South Asia and the World*, New Delhi: Pearson Longman, 2007, pp. 186-189.
14   Ibid, pp. 190-192.
15   Report of Officials of the Governments of India and People's Republic of China on Boundary Issue (Part 3), Ministry of External Affairs, pp. 7-8. http://www.archieve.claudearpi.net/maintenance/uploaded_pics/OR_Part_3.pdf (accessed 28 December 2018)
16   "Sino-Indian Border Dispute at Aksai Chin: A Middle Path For Resolution". *Journal of Development Alternatives and Area Studies*, Volume 25, Number 3, 2006, pp. 6-8.
17   Bansal, op. cit., p. 173.
18   Fishcher et al, op. cit., pp. 64-65.
19   Banerji, op. cit., pp. 190-191.
20   Kaul, op. cit., p. 77.
21   Ibid, p. 219.
22   Woodman, Dorothy, *Himalayan Frontiers: A Political Review of British, Chinese, Indian and Russian Rivalries*, Barrie & Jenkins: 1969, pp. 101 and 360.
23   Bansal, op. cit., p. 174.
24   Ibid, pp. 174-175.
25   Joe Thomas Karackattu, "India–China Border Dispute: Boundary-Making and Shaping of Material Realities from the Mid-Nineteenth to Mid-Twentieth Century", *Journal of the Royal Asiatic Society*, Vol. 18, p. 6.
26   Verma, op. cit.
27   Fishcher et al, op. cit., p. 101.
28   Bansal, op. cit., p. 175.
29   Neville Maxwell, *India's China War*, New York: Pantheon, 1970, p. 3.
30   AG Noorani, "Facts of History", A.G. *Frontline*, Vol. 26, No. 18, 30 August – 12 September 2003.
31   Claude Arpi, "Nehru's Aksai Chin Blunder", Rediff.com, Feb. 3 2017, https://www.rediff.com/news/column/nehrus-aksai-chin-

blunder/20170203.htm (accessed on 28 December 2018).
32. Ibid.
33. PJS Sandhu, Vinay Shankar, DW Dwivedi, *1962: A View From the Other Side of the Hill*, pp 13-37.
34. Demchok is not exactly in Aksai Chin, but for the purpose of this chapter, the entire territory under Chinese occupation in Eastern Ladakh has been considered as Aksai Chin.
35. Kaul, op. cit., p. 152.
36. Hermann Kreutzmann, "Ethnic minorities and marginality in the Pamirian Knot: survival of Wakhi and Kirghiz in a harsh environment and global contexts", *The Geographical Journal*, Vol. 169, No. 3, September 2003, p. 224.
37. Excerpts of the telegram from Jawaharlal Nehru to the British Prime Minister, Clement Attlee; https://www.mtholyoke.edu/acad/intrel/kasnehru.htm (accessed on 28 December 2018).
38. The Boundary Agreement between China and Pakistan, 1963, http://people.unica.it/annamariabaldussi/files/2015/04/China-Pakistan-1963.pdf (accessed on 28 December 2018).
39. M Taylor Fravel, *Strong Borders Secure Nation: Cooperation and Conflict in China's Territorial Disputes*. Princeton: Princeton University Press, 2008, pp. 116-117.
40. Secret note of Captain Younghusband, 2.11.1904, accessed from declassified files, Archives of India, PR_000001260765 (accessed on 2 January 2020).
41. Report of Officials of the Governments of India and People's Republic of China on Boundary issue (Part 3), op. cit., p. 26.
42. The Boundary Agreement Between China and Pakistan, 1963, pp. 251, Legal Documents on Jammu and Kashmir, ISBN 9788193480809 (accessed on 22/12/2019).
43. Ibid.
44. Ibid.
45. Ibid.
46. The Raskam Question, File no PR_000005014350, National Archives of India (accessed on 2 January 2020).
47. Notes accessed from 'Approval of boundary of Kashmir frontier...report', 1930, declassified file no PR_000004002075 (accessed on 2 January 2020).
48. Kaul, op. cit., p. 152.
49. M Nazif Shahrani, *The Kirghiz and Wakhi of Afghanistan: Adaptation to Closed Frontiers and War*, pp. 35-36.
50. 1911 Encyclopedia Britannica. https://www.studylight.org/

encyclopedias/bri/p/pamirs.html.
51. *The Sino-Indian Boundary*, New Delhi: The Indian Society of International Law, 1962, pp. 1-2.
52. Treaty of Chushul, http://www.tibetjustice.org/materials/treaties/treaties3.html (accessed 20 December 2019).
53. Kaul, op. cit., pp. 72-74.
54. Report of the Officials of the Government of India and the People's Republic of China on the Boundary Question (Part 3), op. cit.
55. John Bray, Ladakhi and Bhutanese enclaves in Tibet; http://himalaya.socanth.cam.ac.uk/collections/journals/jbs/pdf/JBS_26_01.pdf (accessed 20 December 2019).
56. Claude Arpi, Demchok and the new silk route: China's double standard, April 1, 2015, http://claudearpi.blogspot.com/search?q=Minsar accessed on 20.12.2019
57. Claude Arpi, "Indian Village in Tibet", Rediff.com, https://www.rediff.com/news/special/the-indian-village-in-tibet/20180213.htm (accessed on 30 Dec 2018).

7

Shrines in Occupied Territories

This chapter deals with various shrines of significance in the occupied territories. People are generally aware of the revered Sharda Peeth, but are not so aware of other places of reverence. The location of shrines clearly indicates that the culture of the region is similar to that of other parts of Ladakh and Jammu and Kashmir. As territory under Chinese occupation is generally devoid of habitation, these shrines are generally located in POJK and POTL. The chapter describes the shrines of minority communities.

Shrines, Temples and Gurudwaras in POJK (Mirpur Muzaffarabad)

Pakistan invaded Jammu and Kashmir State on 20 October 1947. The raids continued and when UN mandated ceasefire was imposed on 1 Jan 1949, Pakistan retained control of the territories it had occupied. During the invasions, which were very brutal, thousands of Non-

Muslims were killed, scores were converted and thousands escaped to areas of Jammu-Kashmir under Indian control. Many temples and shrines had been broken post 1359, when Islamic invasions started in earnest. However, many temples and shrines were still functioning during Maharaja's rule and faced sudden closure, after the area came under Pakistan's occupation. The information about existing temples and shrines in POJK is very sketchy as the area is almost completely Muslim.

Sharda Temple and University

The most well-known shrine in the entire region is undoubtedly, the temple of Goddess Sharda. From ancient times Kashmir was known as Shardapeeth, meaning abode of the goddess Sharda. One of the eighteen Maha Shakti Peethas, Sharada Peeth represents the spiritual location of the goddess Sati's fallen right hand. Sharada Peeth is one of the three holiest sites of pilgrimage for Kashmiri Pandits, along with the Martand Sun Temple and the Amarnath Temple.[1] Sharda is the goddess of learning and for centuries Kashmir was the seat of higher learning. According to Sir George Grierson (1851-1941) author of " linguistic survey of India, "For up to two thousand years Kashmir has been the house of Sanskrit learning and from this small valley they have issued masterpieces of history, poetry, romance, fable and philosophy." Alberuni (973-1048 CE), famous Persian mathematician and astrologer, who visited India wrote in his travel account kitab-ul Hind that "Benaras and Kashmir are two great centres of Hindu Science. It is Kashmir that has produced the greatest historians, poets and philosophers'[2]

The only shrine of the Goddess Sharda—The goddess of learning, in the subcontinent, it was considered as the epitome of religious learning.[3] The ancient temple of Sharda is located in Kishanganga (Neelum) Valley, in Sharda Sub-Division of the Neelum Valley District. It is located in a small village called Shardi or Sardi near the confluence of Kishanganga and Madhumati rivers. It is about 40 miles North West of Wular Lake as the crow flies. A pre-partition account of the shrine states:

> The shrine of Sharda is situated in the Keram-Kishanganga valley at a hillock across the Kishanganga River on the bank of Madhumati, which joins it near the shrine. Surrounded by snow-capped mountains and dense forests, it commands a panoramic view.[4]

The shrine has been described as having a gateway through an impressive staircase with flanking walls, which had 64 big steps and 300 small steps. The big steps were twelve feet long, two feet wide and eighteen inches thick. From top of the stairs a good view of the surroundings was visible. The shrine occupied four kanals of land, of which two were filled with stone. At the centre of the stone floor was the stone temple. There was a *dharmshala* around it. The roof was made up of wood.[5] At present the stair case survives with only sixty three steps.[6]

There were numerous other smaller temples and places of Hindu worship around the temple. Till 1948, there was a regular Shardapeeth Yatra, which started on Ganga Ashtami. The devotees would visit the temple during navratras as well. Punjabi khatris would come and perform *havan* and sacrifice goats on Ashtami. Later due to intervention of a famous Sanyasin Mathra Devi, the goat sacrifice was shifted to Navami. Other places pilgrims and devotees would stop at, were the various 'nags' or water springs/small lakes around the area. The main *nag* was Mukhsar, where on Sapta Babashi water would flow out like pearls. Lord Ram is said to have bathed in the *nag*. Another *nag* of veneration was Maharudra Nag. There are numerous old broken temples around the area. Many *nags* have Stone idols placed in the spring. The yatras continued till Pakistan Occupied the Territory.[7]

During the reign of Kanishka, Sharda was the largest academic institution in Central Asia. It imparted education on Buddhist religion, history, geography, structural science, logic and philosophy. It also evolved a script of its own known as Sharda script. The University was constructed by Kanishka from north to south on a rectangular pedestal and was totally different from other ancient buildings in the sub-continent. According to historical evidence, around 5000 people resided at Sharda.[8] A key source of mythological knowledge about the shrine is the Sharada Sahasranama manuscript, written in the Sharada script, and communicated by Prakash Swami, the last Purohit (or chief priest) of the Sharada temple before the Partition of India.[9]

The earliest available references to Sharada Peeth are found in the Nilamata Purana (6th-8th century CE). In the 10th century, Al-Beruni in his book describes Sharda as being situated in the South-West of Srinagar, considered extremely holy by Indians, where on the eve of Baisakhi, people come from all over India for pilgrimage. He laments the fact he could not visit it due to snow and extremely difficult terrain.[10] He adds that the shrine is venerated by both locals and pilgrims, describing it alongside famous temples of the time such as the Multan Sun Temple and the Somnath temple, suggesting that at that time, Sharada Peeth was among the most revered places of worship in India. Besides, Al-Beruni, Abul Fazal, Bilhana and Kalhana have also described Sharda. In his description of Pravapura (present-day Srinagar), the 11th century poet Bilhana mentions Sharada Peeth, referring to it as the source of Kashmir's reputation as a centre of learning. In Kalhana's 12th century CE work Rajatarangini, he describes Sharada Peeth as a site venerated by Hindus. It is at this temple that Adi Shankaracharya received the right to sit on the Sarvanjnanapeetham (Throne of Wisdom). The first verse of 'Prapanchsar' composed by Adi Shankaracharya is devoted to the praise of Sharada. The Sharada image at Shringeri Sharadamba temple in South India was once said to have been made of sandalwood, which is said to have been taken by Shankaracharya from here. The Vaishnava saint Swami Ramanuja traveled all the way from Srirangam to refer to Bodhayana's vritti on Brahma Sutras preserved here, before commencing work on writing his commentary on the Brahma sutras, the Sri Bhasya. Traditions passed down through centuries point to existence of a great centre of learning at Sharda. Sharada Peeth figures in a number of South Indian traditions, such as the ritual prostration in the direction of Sharada Peeth at the beginning of formal education. Saraswat Brahmin communities in Karnataka

THE DIRECTORATE GENERAL OF TOURISM & ARCHAEOLOGY
AZAD GOVT. OF THE STATE OF JAMMU & KASHMIR

No:

Dated:

Circular.

On the humble request of Save Sharda Community Kashmir (Regd) New Dehli, Headed by Mr. Ravinder Pandita sent a Email for save Sharda Pilgrim, Mr. Ravider also suggested for sanctity of the shrine and 2,Nos awareness sign boards, should be installed, one at the entry near stairs of Sharda Premises and other before entering the temple (Sanctum Sanctorum) by these sign boards, the visitors should be made aware to put off their shoes before entering the Temple, to maintain religious sanctity being a religious place of Kashmir Pandits. Keeping in view being a Muslim and a religious Nation we are bound to protect and secured of this historical shrine. In this regard Supreme Court of Azad Jammu and Kashmir secured a order no Sc/2017 dated 03-01-2018 as well.

Director General
Tourism & Archaeology,
GoAJ&K

No 9973-80 Dated 31/12/18

Copy to:-

1. PS to The Secretary Tourism and Information GoAJK.
2. BM 5-AK Brigade for information.
3. Comanding Officer 33 FF for information.
4. Deputy Commissioner Nellum for information and implementation.
5. SSP Nellum for information.
6. Assistant Director Tourism District Nellum for implementation.
7. Assistant Director Archaeology Mzd, for necessary action.
8. Mr Ravindar Pandita Head of Save Sharda Community (Reg)

Director General
Tourism & Archaeology
GoAJ&K

OCCUPIED TERRITORIES OF BHARAT

REGISTRAR
SUPREME COURT OF
AZAD JAMMU & KASHMIR

Muzaffarabad
Tele: Off: 05822-929711
Fax No: 929713
No SC/ /2017
Dated: 03.01.2018

To

Dear Mr. Ravinder Pandita,
Founder Save Sharda Committee,
<u>Kashmir (Regd.)</u>

Your letter addressed to Mr. Justice Chaudhary Muhammad Ibrahim Zia, the Hon'ble Chief Justice of Azad Jammu & Kashmir was placed before his Lordship on the 2nd day of January, 2018. I have been directed to convey that already this Court in the cases reported as Rehmat ullah Khan & 3 others Vrs. Azad Govt. & 3 others (2014 SCR 1358) and Azad Govt. & 5 others Vrs. Ghulam Nabi Shah (2015 SCR 816) has been pleased to issue direction to the State Authorities for protection of the Religious **Places and Symbols** such as Temples and Gordwara etc. You may approach the concerned State Authorities seeking remedy as claimed by you in the letter. In case failure on the part of State functionaries in carrying out of the judgments you may approach this Court for redressal of your grievance. (The copies of judgments for perusal and further action are enclosed herewith as annexures "A&B").

The Honourable Chief Justice of Azad Jammu & Kashmir has appreciated the efforts of your **committee** for humanity. It is expected that the committee shall not confine itself only to restoration of the places relating to a specific religion but also shall focus on restoration and **protection of the Holy Places and** symbols of the other Religions. It is also desired that **the committee** shall raise voice against worst fanatic acts like demolishing **of the Babri Masjid in Ayudhta** and the religious places of other religions especially the **buildings and sacred** places relating to the religion of **Islam**.

RIAZ AHMED
REGISTRAR

are said to perform a ritual of moving seven steps towards Kashmir before retracing their steps during the *yagnopavit* ceremony. Pan Bharat Sharada Stotram is a part of morning prayers *"Namaste Sarada Devi Kashmira mandala vasini"*.[11]

Current Status

Post 1947, when Pakistan invaded Kashmir and occupied Neelum valley, Swami Nandlal Ji, who was the priest of Sharda Peeth, carried Idols from Shrada Peeth to Kupwara. At present some idols are in Devibal at Baramulla and some in Tikker at Kupwara. Save Sharda Committee Kashmir (SSCK) under Ravinder Pandita has been in the forefront of the efforts to save Sharda Peeth and start prayers and pilgrimages there. There has been contact with civil society members in Neelum Valley. Consequently, flowers were offered at the shrine on 2 November 2016 by civil society members of Neelum. A picture of Sharda Devi was installed in the shrine on 3 March 2017 and soil and flowers from the shrine were sent to India.[12] The SSCK then distributed the soil to the Shankaracharayas of the four *mutts* in India. In February 19, at the Kumbh Mela, a resolution was passed by all four Shankaracharayas for reopening of Sharda pilgrimage. In March 19, Pakistani media reported that the Pakistani Government is examining the opening of Sharada Peeth. However, no progress has been made. These are important milestones in the battle to reclaim Sharda Peeth, a temple and a university which was as great as Nalanda.[13]

Other Temples and Shrines

Mirpur city had many temples, most of which got submerged when Mangla Dam was constructed. Mangla Devi Temple apparently is visible when water levels are low in Mangla Dam. Travel books like Trip Adviser talk about a Shivala temple and Banganga temple at Mirpur, but no other information is available on them. Similarly, there was a Devi Gali temple near Poonch in POJK. Devi Gali has lush green grassy grounds surrounded by dense pine forest and mountains. The name Devi Gali is linked to this area's history. According to locals, this spot was a place of worship for Hindus, years before occupation of the area by Pakistan.

Ali Baig Gurdwara, a popular place of worship for Sikhs in Ali Baig village, has been turned by the POJK authorities into the Muhammad Yaqoob Shaheed High School for Girls. Located on the northeastern side of the Mirpur-Jhelum link road in Bhimber tehsil, the three-storey building also served as a refugee camp for three years, then a police station, a soap factory and a primary school for girls. The gurdwara's domes have been decorated with lotus flowers and can be seen from a distance.

In 2014, efforts were made to document archaeological sites in Pakistan Occupied Jammu Kashmir. About 100 sites were documented in Muzaffarabad Division. During the survey, monuments including Thorchi Fort, Sharda Fort, Chak Fort, Barnad Fort, Aion Fort Ranbir Singh Baradari, Hindu temples, rock-cut sanctuaries, Nagara, Baradari, wells, Ali Baig Gurdwara and rock boulders with historical

SHRINES IN OCCUPIED TERRITORIES

impressions were documented. Researchers found that most of them had become shelters for stray animals and drug addicts.[14] Ramkot Fort in Mirpur District near Mangla dam is built over ancient temples. Excavations have proven existence of temples.[15]

Shrines in Gilgit Baltistan (POTL)

Gilgit Baltistan's pre Islamic past lives on in monuments, rock carvings and artefacts being recovered daily. There are monuments dating back to Emperor Ashoka and earlier. The proofs of a rich Hindu and Buddhist heritage lie scattered around the trade routes and passes. Karakoram road from Hunza to Chilas has nearly ten thousand rock carvings. There is not much official information about the sites and they lie in ruins. About 30,000 petroglyphs and 5000 graffiti have been discovered in and around the ancient trade routes in Gilgit-Baltistan. These have been preserved by A natural process termed as 'Desert Patina'.

Brahmi, Kharosti, Sogdian, Bactrian, Tibetan and Hebrew inscriptions provide valuable inputs on the cultural and linguistic interactions along the trade routes. A Brahmi inscription from Hunza-Haldeikish records "Balamitra from Mathura Arrived here"[16] According to old scripts the ancient names of the main towns in Gilgit Baltistan were Chilas-Shilathasa, Shiltas, Gilgit-Gidagitti (great city) where eight stone 'samgrahams' indicated Buddhism was flourishing. The ancient cultural linkages are strewn around in Gilgit Baltistan as a testimony of its Links with Bharat.[17] The major Buddhist shrines are mentioned below

Kargah Buddha

Kargah Buddha is an archaeological site located about 6 miles (9.7 km) outside of Gilgit. It is a carved image of a large standing Buddha, some 50 feet high, in the cliff-face in Karghah Nala. The carving, which is in a style also found in Baltistan, probably dates to the 7th century. In Shina language, spoken in Gilgit it is called Yshani or Yakshini. The shrine is accessed by a badly maintained road and is not maintained. [18]

Manthal Buddha Rock

Manthal Buddha Rock is a large granite rock on which picture of Lord Buddha is engraved which probably dates back to 8th century. This rock is located in Manthal village near Skardu Town. Buddha Rock is one of the most important relics of Buddhism in Skardu. It's about three kilometres from Sadpara Road. Sadpara road leads to Satpara Lake. The Buddha carving was not known to the world till beginning of 20th century due to its remote location. In 1906 the Scottish traveller Ella Christie wrote a book on her journey to the Western Tibet and featured the carving in her book which gave it an international attention. Shedding light on the ancient relief, historian Muhammad Abbas Kazmi says the carving and Tibetan inscriptions were made on a 30-foot high and 20-foot wide triangle-shaped rock. "The carving depicts present time Buddha—Siddhartha Gautama—in the centre, 20 smaller Buddhas of the past around him and future Buddhas—Maitreya—standing on both sides," Kazmi interprets. He claims that in Buddhist tradition, the 'Council of all Buddhas' as

SHRINES IN OCCUPIED TERRITORIES

Statue of Lord Buddha at Kargah Nalla, 10 KM from Gilgit. The statue discovered in 1938, after the discovery of Gilgit manuscripts in 1931 is the most well-known monument near Gilgit

Distant view of Kargah Buddha. Pakistan's National Flag can be seen flying over the statue. It would have been impossible to fly the flag, if it was an Islamic shrine

Manthal Buddha: A large granite rock on which picture of Lord Buddha is engraved dating back to 8th Century, at Manthal village, just outside Skardu

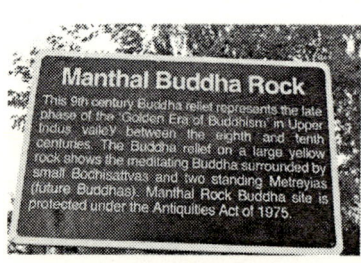

Manthal Buddha Rock Inscription

Buddhist Stupa built between 8th and 10th Century AD

represented in the carving is called 'Mandal' – a word from which the village's name is derived. Since then the government has taken many steps to preserve this monument and it is visited by tourists who visit the Skardu city.[19]

Other Buddhist Shrines

There are ruins of an ancient stupa near Henzel, a small town in Gilgit area of Gilgit Baltistan whose main claim to fame is the ruined Stupa. Rock Inscriptions are an archaeological site in Danyor, Gilgit-Baltistan. It is a gigantic boulder bearing inscriptions from the 7-8th century AD during the reign of Navasurendradityanandi.[20] The site is located on the left bank of the Gilgit River along the Karakoram Highway Road in Danyor.

The Sacred Rock of Hunza is a carved rock as well as a cultural heritage site that dates back to the 1st Millennium AD. The sacred rock is located in place called Haldeikish near to the small town of Karimabad in Hunza Valley. The site is on top of a Hill which is at the left bank of the river Hunza. The rock is 30 feet high and 200 yards long. It is easily accessible from the Karakoram Highway which connects Pakistan with China. It is an isolated rock which is further divided into two portions. The rock is divided into two parts, once there used to be some Buddhist shelter caves which fell over time. The rock is one of the major tourist attractions in Gilgit-Baltistan.[21]

There are more than 50,000 pieces of Buddhist rock art (petroglyphs) and inscriptions all along the Karakoram

Highway in Gilgit-Baltistan. These are concentrated at ten major sites between Hunza and Shatial, more have been found in the area of Skardu and Shigar (in Shigar even the remains of a Buddhist monastery were found in 1984 by Jettmar and Thewalt). The carvings were left by various invaders, traders and pilgrims who passed along the trade route, as well as by locals. The earliest carvings date back to between 5000 and 1000 BC, showing single animals, triangular men and hunting scenes in which the animals sometimes are larger than the hunters. These carvings were carved into the rocks with stone tools and are covered with a thick patina that proves their age. Later—mostly Buddhist—carvings were sometimes executed with a sharp chisel.[22] There are also engravings depicting Lord Krishna and Balaram in Chilas.[23]

Gurudwara in Skardu

Gurudwara Chota Nanakiana at Skardu is believed to have been visited by Guru Nanak Dev, the founder of Sikh religion. He had stayed at this place while he was on his way back from China. It is also called as "Asthan Nanak Pir" by the local people. It is located at a distance of two kilometres from Skardu Fort. Every year thousands of people come to visit this place in summer. There is a big building on top of a small hill (about 1 km from the main cross road of Skardu). It is this building which is known as Gurdwara Chota Nanakiana. Prakashasthan (congregation hall), langar (community kitchen) hall, and inn for pilgrims are on the hill. There are several shops on the main road below this building. These shops are owned by this sacred place. The building is not in a good condition, Prakash asthan has started collapsing and rest of the building too wears a deserted look. Only the shops remain as they are looked after by the occupants.[24]

NOTES

1. Ramesh Kumar, "Sarada Pilgrimage - its Socio-Historicity - I", *Kashmir Sentinel*, 16 December 1998 – 15 January 1999, p. 16. (Retrieved on 29/12/2019)
2. Bansi Pandit, "Explore Kashmiri Pandits', Dharma Publications, 2008, pp. 77-93, ISBN 0963479865
3. There is another Shardsa temple in Maihar in Madhya Pradesh, but that appears to be have come up much later, The temple in Neelum Valley was the only Sharda Temple in ancient time.
4. AR Nazki, "Sharda: History and Importance" in K Warikoo (ed), The Other Kashmir: Society, Culture and Politics in the Karakoram Himalayas. New Delhi: Pentagon Press, 2014, pp. 35-37.
5. Ibid, p. 37.
6. Ibid, pp. 37-38.
7. Sonalal, "A witness to Sharda Yatras" *Kashmir Sentinel*, 16 December 1998 – 15 January 1999 (retrieved on 29/12/2019)
8. AR Nazki, n. 4, p. 38.
9. Brij Nath Tikkoo, (2010). Shri Sharada Mahatmya. Ajmer: Vikas Printing Press. pp. (ii), 1, 7–13.
10. AR Nazki, n. 4, p. 38.
11. Abode of Goddess Sharda at Shardi, Brigadier Rattan Kaul https://web.archive.org/web/20181221033803/http://koausa.org/temples/sharda3.html
12. POK muslims send sacred soil to Kashmiri Pandits, 11 January 2017 https://www.dnaindia.com/lifestyle/report-pok-muslims-send-sacred-soil-to-kashmiri-pandits-2291214 accessed on 29/12/2019
13. Acknowledgement for this information to Sri Ravinder Pandita Ji, founder and president of Save Sharda Committee Kashmir.
14. Seminar: Archeologists urge preservation of Monuments in Azad Kashmir, Jan 2, 2014 https://tribune.com.pk/story/653419/seminar-archaeologists-urge-preservation-of-monuments-in-azad-kashmir/ accessed on 29/12/2019
15. Ramkot Fort, centuries old Kashmiri heritage site on verge of

destruction, Jan 29, 2012 https://tribune.com.pk/story/328768/ramkot-fort-centuries-old-kashmiri-heritage-site-on-the-verge-of-destruction/ accessed on 29/12/2019

16. Jason Neelis, "Capillary Routes of the Upper Indus." In Early Buddhist Transmission and Trade Networks: Mobility and Exchange within and beyond the Northwestern Borderlands of South Asia, 257-88. LEIDEN; BOSTON: Brill, 2011. Accessed January 15, 2020. www.jstor.org/stable/10.1163/j.ctt1w8h16r.11.
17. Ibid
18. https://thehighasia.com/buddhist-treasure-in-gilgit-cries-out-for-govts-attention/ Buddhist treasure in Asia calls out for Govt Attention, High Asia, July 8, 2019, accessed on 29/12/2019.
19. In Skardu, Siddarth Sings On, Feriya Ilyas, July 26, 2015, *The Tribune*, https://tribune.com.pk/story/922014/in-skardu-siddhartha-sings-on/ accessed on 29/12/2019
20. Gudrun Melzer, A Palaeographic Study of a Buddhist Manuscript from the Gilgit-Baltistan Region, op. cit.
21. https://unesdoc.unesco.org/ark:/48223/pf0000042046 Rock carvings at the sacred rock of Hunza, PDF Accessed on 10 January 2020, p. 2.
22. Jason Neelis, "Capillary Routes of the Upper Indus." In Early Buddhist Transmission and Trade Networks: Mobility and Exchange within and beyond the Northwestern Borderlands of South Asia, 257-88. LEIDEN; BOSTON: Brill, 2011. Accessed January 15, 2020. www.jstor.org/stable/10.1163/j.ctt1w8h16r.11, op. cit.
23. https://en.m.wikipedia.org/wiki/Chilas#/media/File%3ARama_Krishna_at_Chilas.jpg
24. https://www.sikhdharma.org/gurdwara-bhai-biba-singh/ Gurudwara in Skardu, accessed 29/12/2019

8

Conclusion

The issue of Occupied territories under foreign occupation is of great national importance. This issue has been consigned to dark corners of national consciousness. There is a veil of darkness and ignorance about the occupied territories. The Issue of 1962 defeat is a part of national psyche, but strangely there is no discussion regarding the regions under Chinese occupation as a result of the war. Gilgit Baltistan is another region totally under a veil of darkness. Minsar is totally unknown except to those minuscule people doing academic studies of the region. Though terror launch pads, Kargil War, incursions across LOC are news headlines, strangely they have never been linked to Pakistan occupied territories which enable these events. Trans-Karakorum Tracts draw a void in national Awareness. The only issue in limelight is the so called plebiscite in Kashmir valley, totally de linked from the issue of Pakistan occupying large swathes of territory of the erstwhile state of Jammu and Kashmir.

Parliament issued a resolution on 24 February 1994, stating that territories under foreign occupation are part of India and that the government is committed to bringing them back within Indian fold. Yet there is no annual marking and reiteration of the same resolution. It is imperative that these regions are made into national issues.

From the very moment of its birth, Pakistan has made 'Kashmir' a central pillar of its strategic quest, linked integrally to the fundamentals of its long-emergent and tenuous national identity. Across successive governments, through 'democratic' and military regimes, a relentless 'Kashmir policy' has been followed.

In international fora, Pakistan has established its narrative on Kashmir as a part of Pakistan and made issue of plebiscite in Indian controlled Kashmir valley an international issue. Pakistan and China entered into a nexus, with Pakistan ceding Trans-Karakorum Tracts to China. This enabled both the occupying nations to encircle and contain India, isolating it from the geopolitical developments in most of Eurasian landmass.

Pakistan has indulged in demographic engineering in occupied territory of Gilgit Baltistan by repealing the state subject rule, while demanding plebiscite in Indian part of Kashmir. The propaganda of Pakistan has been so successful that these issues have never been highlighted.

Pakistan indulges in repression of ethnic communities in the occupied regions but these issues have never been mainstreamed, either domestically or internationally.

CONCLUSION

Pakistan has successfully managed to delink the issue of Gilgit Baltistan from the issue of Kashmir. The challenge is to link the Kashmir issue with Areas under Pakistani occupation. By creating a union territory of Ladakh and including the area of Gilgit Baltistan in Ladakh, historical linkages have been re-explored, legitimising Indian claim over the territory.

There has been a tendency amongst policy makers in India to treat the issue of Gilgit-Baltistan and Aksai Chin as a dead issue, with a tendency to support status quo. Many policy makers have supported a compromise by advocating that the LOC be turned into International border and to let Pakistan and China keep the occupied territories. These recommendations expose the ignorance of the strategic importance of the occupied territories.

The Indian narrative has to focus on the events of 1947-1949, expose how, till the ceasefire came into effect, the areas now under occupation were parts of India where Indian Army was fighting to clear Indian territory of foreign nationals and Pakistani Army. The horrors suffered by the non Muslim population of areas under Pakistan's illegal occupation need to be revisited and be bought into public domain. The Hypocrisy of UN resolutions need to be exposed, as also the dead 'Plebiscite' which has become the identity of the Indo-Pak Kashmir issue. A clear understanding of the Part 2 of the UN resolution of 13 August 1948 (based on UNCIP recommendation) has to be communicated. The only working part of the UN resolution is the acceptance of Pakistan forces on Indian soil, and the need for them to vacate occupied territories. The defence minister and home minister of India have made it very clear to Pakistan that any talk on Kashmir will be on Pakistan vacating Occupied Territories.

The strategic significance of vassal states of Jammu and Kashmir has never been clearly understood. The British appreciated their significance. In 1891, they helped Maharaja to conquer Hunza and Nagar. After that, they created a Gilgit Agency to ward off threats from Russia and China. They understood the importance of securing the frontiers and entered into negotiations with China and Russia. The main endeavour of British was to control the external frontiers consisting of vassal states. A secret note of British now declassified states "the reason why there should be central control of Kashmir's frontier remains valid, the state is contiguous with Afghanistan(with Soviet Turkestan only a few miles distant), the Chinese province of Sinkiang and Tibet, and is a focal point which might become very important to India"[1]

The significance of the region is clearly visible with China Pakistan Economic Corridor (CPEC) taking shape and reiterates the British policy of treating the area with special interest. It is true that the matters were taken out of India's hands by the invasion of Jammu and Kashmir by armed raiders backed by Pakistan Army, the mutiny in Maharaja's forces and subsequently, the 'accession' of vassal states.

The UN, though professing to safeguard peace, has paid

CONCLUSION

lip service to the issue of occupation, letting it get supplemented by the issue of plebiscite. The US started giving aid to Pakistan in early 1950's, and entered into military pacts to with it, have access to Afghanistan. UK, though professing to uphold sanctity of UN resolutions, supported the construction of Mangla Dam, which altered the Demography of Mirpur. China, since 1962, has constantly helped Pakistan to break UN resolutions by entering into Sino Pak boundary agreement, then by construction of Karakoram Highway and now by the ongoing projects associated with CPEC.

The Chinese occupied territories excluding Shaksgam are not under UNSC resolutions. The issue of Aksai Chin is a British Legacy. Though Territory has been occupied by China, it remains a bilateral issue. There can be a solution found taking present realities and traditional ancient claims in to account. China closed ancient trade routes that existed in Ladakh with Central Asia and Tibet, while creating a new route by building the Aksai Chin Highway. This has caused isolation and encirclement of Ladakh, while hijacking the existing trade routes that Ladakh had with Tibet and Central Asia. China and Pakistan are attempting the creation of a new trade route through CPEC. Already India has been cut off from Central Asia, Afghanistan and Eurasian heartland. The CPEC, like the Aksai Chin Highway, also creates a military threat for India.

The secret papers now declassified regarding the publishing of Map of 1930 offer interesting insights on the Kashmir frontiers in the north and the Indo -Tibetan

Frontier north of Bhutan. The letter from India Office, Whitehall, dated 28 February 1930, explicitly states that the new border will be according to the Anglo-Tibet Simla agreement of 1913 and that puts Aksai chin firmly in India's borders, as had been the case with Johnson line and Johnson-Ardagh line. The MacDonald-Macartney line had been used for a very little time, and had been abandoned by the British themselves. There is a need to rationalise the boundary agreements. The reality of the Aksai Chin Highway, the easier accessibility of the now closed routes, the desirability for India to have land access to Central Asia, all are various paradigms of the problem. The older routes were created through centuries of travel, and catered to the needs of availability of food for livestock. Now with travel being done in vehicles, need is of fuel and rest houses. In olden days, boundaries were marked on Maps and not on ground for vast areas, and often physical landmarks were not factored in. In today's world of satellite maps, mapping boundaries taking into account physical landmarks, watersheds, passes, etc will be much easier. China has not been able to produce any real claim to Aksai chin or Trans-Karakoram tracts, and is occupying it by virtue of its military might. India needs to become strident on its traditional, ancient claims, especially regarding the traditional route to Kailash Mansarovar, which for centuries has been the most important pilgrimage for Indians.

Need of the present is to make the issue of occupied territories of Bharat a national issue. The public has to understand how Bharat was strong and prosperous because

CONCLUSION

of access to these areas. The narrative of status quo regarding these areas as a lost cause needs to be changed.

NOTE

1. 'The Question of surrender by Jammu Kashmir state to the centre the effective control and administration of External frontiers and taking over Ladakh tehsil' File no PR_000004001182, national archives of India, accessed on 2 January 2020.

APPENDICES

Appendix A

UNCIP Resolution of August 13, 1948
(S/1100, Para 75)

The United Nations Commission for India and Pakistan having given careful consideration to the points of view expressed by the Representatives of India and Pakistan regarding the situation in the State of Jammu and Kashmir, and

Being of the opinion that the prompt cessation of hostilities and the correction of conditions the continuance of which is likely to endanger international peace and security are essential to implementation of its endeavours to assist the Governments of India and Pakistan in effecting a final settlement of the situation,

Resolves to submit simultaneously to the Governments of India and Pakistan the following proposal:

PART I: CEASE-FIRE ORDER

A. The Governments of India and Pakistan agree that their respective High Commands will issue separately and simultaneously a cease-fire order to apply to all forces under their control in the State of Jammu and Kashmir as of the earliest practicable date or dates to be mutually agreed upon within four days after these proposals have been accepted by both Governments.

B. The High Commands of the Indian and Pakistani forces agree to refrain from taking any measures that might augment the military potential of the forces under their control in the State of Jammu and Kashmir.

(For the purpose of these proposals "forces under their control" shall be considered to include all forces, organized and unorganized, fighting or participating in hostilities on their respective sides.)

C. The Commander-in-Chief of the forces of India and Pakistan shall promptly confer regarding any necessary local changes in present dispositions which may facilitate the cease-fire.

D. In its discretion and as the Commission may find practicable, the Commission will appoint military observers who, under the authority of the Commission and with the cooperation of both Commands, will supervise the observance of the cease-fire order.

E. The Government of India and the Government of Pakistan agree to appeal to their respective peoples to assist in creating and maintaining an atmosphere favourable to the promotion of further negotiations.

PART II: TRUCE AGREEMENT

Simultaneously with the acceptance of the proposal for the immediate cessation of hostilities as outlined in Part 1, both Governments accept the following principles as a basis for the formulation of a truce agreement, the details of which shall be worked out in discussion between their Representatives and the Commission.

UNCIP RESOLUTION OF AUGUST 13, 1948

A 1. As the presence of troops of Pakistan in the territory of the State of Jammu and Kashmir constitutes a material change in the situation since it was represented by the Government of Pakistan before the Security Council, the Government of Pakistan agrees to withdraw its troops from that State.

2. The Government of Pakistan will use its best endeavour to secure the withdrawal from the State of Jammu and Kashmir of tribesmen and Pakistan nationals not normally resident therein who have entered the State for the purpose of fighting.

3. Pending a final solution, the territory evacuated by the Pakistani troops will be administered by the local authorities under the surveillance of the Commission.

B 1. When the Commission shall have notified the Government of India that the tribesmen and Pakistan nationals referred to in Part IIA2 hereof have withdrawn, thereby terminating the situation which was represented by the Government of India to the Security Council as having occasioned the presence of Indian forces in the State of Jammu and Kashmir, and further, that the Pakistani forces are being withdrawn from the State of Jammu and Kashmir, the Government of India agrees to begin to withdraw the bulk of their forces from that State in stages to be agreed upon with the Commission.

2. Pending the acceptance of the conditions for a final settlement of the situation in the State of Jammu and Kashmir, the Indian Government will maintain within the lines existing at the moment of cease-fire the minimum strength of its forces which in agreement with the Commission are considered necessary to assist local authorities in the observance of law and order. The

Commission will have observers stationed where it deems necessary.

3. The Government of India will undertake to ensure that the Government of the State of Jammu and Kashmir will take all measures within its power to make it publicly known that peace, law and order will be safeguarded and that all human and political rights will be guaranteed.

C 1. Upon signature, the full text of the truce agreement or a communiqué containing the principles thereof as agreed upon between the two Governments and the Commission will be made public.

PART III

The Government of India and the Government of Pakistan reaffirm their wish that the future status of the State of Jammu and Kashmir shall be determined in accordance with the will of the people and to that end, upon acceptance of the truce agreement, both Governments agree to enter into consultations with the Commission to determine fair and equitable conditions whereby such free expression will be assured.

Sourced from http ://www.indianembassy.org/policy/Kashmir/uncip/s(1100).htm

https://web.archive.org/web/20071013165623/http://www.indianembassy.org/policy/Kashmir/uncip%28s1100%29.htm

Appendix B

Karachi Agreement

Heads of agreement between Hon'ble Minister without Portfolio. The President of All Jammu and Kashmir Muslim Conference and the President of the Azad Kashmir Government

Civil Administration and Azad Kashmir Areas

    (i) The Azad Kashmir Cabinet shall formulate policy and generally supervise administration in Azad Kashmir area. Day to day administration hall however, be entrusted to executive officers viz. the Heads of Departments who shall also be secretaries to government for their respective Departments.

    (ii) Besides the Heads of Departments the Azad Kashmir Government will have only the following two secretaries:

        1. Secretary, Finance Department, and

        2. Cabinet Secretary.

    The Cabinet Secretary besides maintaining records

of Cabinet proceedings will be directly responsible to keep the Cabinet well-posted with all matters connected with the plebiscite and for all correspondence with the Plebiscite Administrator.

(iii) The details of the set up will be as follows:

	Subjects	Head of Deptt.-cum-Secretary	Minister Incharge
1.	Law and Order Including Jails and Police	Commissioner-cum-Chief Secretary	Hon'ble president
2.	Food and Civil Supplies	Director of Food and Civil Supplies and Secretary to Government Civil Supplies Deptt.	Minister for Civil Supplies
3.	Revenues (includeing Forests, Customs) and Public Works.	Commissioner-cum-Chief Chief Secretary.	Revenue & Finance Minister
4.	Finance Minister	Finance Secretary	Revenue & Finance
5.	Rehabilitation & Secretary Rehabilitation Deptt.	Director of Rehabilitation	Minister for Rehabilitation
6.	Medical & Health Secretary	Director of Health Services & Health Services	Minister for Health and Education
7.	Education Secretary	Director of Education & Education	Ministry of Health and Education
8.	Cabinet & Plebiscite Works	Cabinet Secretary	Hon'ble President

(iv) No one below the rank of Head of Department/Secretary shall have access to the Ministers and orders to lower staff shall always be communicated through the head of Department/Secretary

(v) Heads of Department/Secretaries shall submit all important cases to their Ministers and shall generally keep them fully informed of developments in their respective Departments.

(vi) Heads of Department/Secretaries who are at present located outside Azad Kashmir area may continue to be so located. But they would meet their Ministers once or twice a week and put up cases on which orders of Ministers have to be obtained.

(vii) Whenever a Head of Department feels that an order passed by an Hon'ble Minister needs revision, he would bring the case to the notice of the Commissioner who in capacity as Chief Secretary to the Azad Kashmir Government, will endeavour to have the matter satisfactory settled, if necessary, in consultation with the Chief Plebiscite Adviser to the Pakistan Government, who will also be notified by the Azad Kashmir Government as their Chief Advisor.

(viii) Officers loaned to Azad Kashmir Government will formally appointed as Officers-on-Specific Duty with the Chief Plebiscite Adviser and their services will informally be placed at the disposal of Azad Kashmir Government who would formally appoint them to office by notification in their own Gazette. All correspondence of the Azad Kashmir Government with the Secretariat of the Minister without Portfolio, Government of Pakistan, will be through the Chief Plebiscite Advisor.

(ix) Pending the appointment of a Public Service Commission for Azad Kashmir an ad hoc Committee consisting of the following may be appointed to recommend future recruitment and promotions in services in Azad Kashmir Government.

    1. Commissioner (Chairman).
    2. Judge of Azad Kashmir High Court.

3. The Head of the Department concerned.
4. Cabinet Secretary as Member-Secretary.

II. Financial Arrangements

(i) Monies advanced to the A.K. Government for specific purposes shall be spent for those purposes and no other. The Pakistan Government shall satisfy themselves that they have been properly spent.

(ii) Moneys advanced to the A.K. Government as general grants-in-aid shall be given only after the A.K. Government has produced a budget statement for the Government as a whole. In the case of these funds, the Government of Pakistan shall satisfy themselves that A.K. Government spend according to the budget proposals. For this purpose, they may ask for periodical statement of account from that Government.

(iii) The Pakistan Government shall loan the services of an Accounts Officer for employment as Accountant General of the Azad Kashmir Government.

III. Division of functions between the Government of Pakistan, The Azad Kashmir Government and the Muslim Conference.

A. Matters within the Purview of Pakistan Government

(i) Defence, (Complete Control over A.K. Government).

(ii) Negotiations with U.N.C.I.P.

(iii) Foreign Policy of A.K. Government.

(iv) Publicity in Pakistan and Foreign Countries.

(v) Coordination of arrangements for relief and rehabilitation of refugees.

(vi) All activities within Pakistan itself with regard to

Kashmir such as procurement of food and civil supplies transport, running of refugee camps, medical arrangements etc.

(vii) All affairs of the Gilgit and Ladakh areas under the control of Political Agent at Gilgit.

B. *Matters within the Purview of A.K. Government*
   (i) Policy with regard to administration in Azad Kashmir.
   (ii) General Supervision of administration in Azad Kashmir.
   (iii) Publicity with regard to activities of the A.K. Government and its administration.
   (iv) Advise to H.M. without portfolio with regard to negotiations with U.N.C.I.P.
   (v) Development of economic resources of A.K. area.

C. *Matters within the Purview of Muslim Conference*
   (i) Publicity with regard to plebiscite in A.K. Government.
   (ii) Field work and publicity in the Indian occupied area of the State.
   (iii) Organisation of political activities in the A.K. and the Indian occupied areas of the State.
   (iv) Preliminary arrangements in connection with plebiscite.
   (v) Organisation for contesting the plebiscite.
   (vi) Political work and publicity among Kashmir refugees in Pakistan.

(vii) General guidance of the A.K. Government.
(viii) Advice to H.M. without portfolio with regard to negotiations with U.N.C.I.P.

Sd/-	Sd/-	Sd/-
(Mohammad Ibrahim)	(Ghulam Abbas)	(M.A. Gurmani)
President Azad Kashmir Govt.	President All Jammu and Muslim Conference	Minister without Portfolio, Govt. of Pakistan.
28/4/49	28/4	

Appendix C

Sino-Pak Boundary Agreement

The Government of the People's Republic of China and the Government of Pakistan; HAVING agreed, with a view to ensuring the prevailing peace and tranquility on their respective border, to formally delimit and demarcate the boundary between China's Sinkiang and the contiguous areas the defence of which is under the actual control of Pakistan, in a spirit of fairness, reasonableness, mutual understanding and mutual accommodation, and on the basis of the ten principles as enunciated in the Bandung conference. Being convinced that this would not only give full expression to the desire of the people of China and Pakistan for the development of good neighbourly and friendly relations, but also help safeguard Asian and world peace.

Have resolved for this purpose to conclude the present agreement and have appointed as their respective plenipotentiaries the following.

For the Government of the People's Republic of China; Chen Yi, Minister of Foreign Affairs.

For the Government of Pakistan Zulfikar Ali Bhutto, Minister of External Affairs.

Who, having mutually examined their full powers and found them to be in good and due form have agreed upon following:

Article 1: In view of the fact that the boundary between China's Sinkiang and the contiguous areas the defence of which is under the actual control of Pakistan has never been formally delimited, two parties agree to delimit it on the basis of the traditional customary boundary line including features and in a spirit of equality, mutual benefit and friendly cooperation.

Article 2: In accordance with the principle expounded in Article 1 of the present agreement, the two parties have fixed as follows the alignment of the entire boundary line between China's Sinkiang and the contiguous areas the defence of which is under the actual control of Pakistan.

1. Commencing from its north western extremity at height 5,630 metres (a peak the reference coordinates of which are approximately longitude 74 degrees 34 minutes east and latitude 37 degrees 3 minutes north), the boundary line runs generally eastward and then South-eastward strictly along the main watershed between the tributaries of the Tashkurgan River of the Tarim river system on the one hand on the tributes of the Hunza river of the Indus river system on the other hand, passing through the Kilik Daban (Dawan), the Mintake Daban (Pass), the Kharchanai Daban (named on the Chinese map only), the Mutsgila Daban (named on the Chinese map only) and the Parpik Pass (named on the

Pakistan map only) and reaches the Khunjerab (Yutr) Daban (Pass).

2 After passing through the Khunjerab (Yutr) Daban (pass) the boundary line runs generally southward along the above-mentioned main watershed up to a mountain-top south of the Daban (pass), where it leaves the main watershed to follow the crest of a spur lying generally in a south-easterly direction, which is the watershed between the Akjilga river (a nameless corresponding river on the Pakistan map) on the one hand, and the Taghumbash (Oprang) river and the Koliman Su (Oprang Jilga) on the other hand. According to the map of the Chinese side, the boundary line, after leaving the south-eastern extremity of the spur, runs along a small section of the middle line of the bed of the Koliman Su to reach its confluence with the Kelechin river. According to the map of the Pakistan side, the boundary line, after leaving the south-eastern extremity of this spur, reaches the sharp bend of the Shaksgam or Muztagh river.

3 From the aforesaid point, the boundary lines runs up the Kelechin river (Shaksgam or Muztagh river) along the middle line of its bed its confluence (reference coordinates approximately longitude 76 degrees 2 minutes east and latitude 36 degrees 26 minutes north) with the Shorbulak Daria (Shimshal river or Braldu river).

4 From the confluence of the aforesaid two rivers, the boundary line, according to the map of the Chinese side, ascends the crest of a spur and runs along it to join the Karakoram range main watershed at a mountain-top (reference coordinates approximately

longitude 75 degrees 54 minutes east and latitude 36 degrees 15 minutes north) which on this map is shown as belonging to the Shorgulak mountain. According to the map of the Pakistan side, the boundary line from the confluence of the above mentioned two river ascends the crest of a corresponding spur and runs along it, passing through height 6.520 meters (21,390 feet) until it joins the Karakoram range main watershed at a peak (reference coordinates approximately longitude 75 degrees 57 minutes east and latitude 36 degrees 3 minutes north).

5 Thence, the boundary line, running generally southward and then eastward strictly follows the Karakoram range main watershed which separates the Tarim river drainage system from the Indus river drainage system, passing through the east Mustagh Pass (Muztagh pass), the top of the Chogri peak (K2) the top of the Broad Peak, the top of the Gasherbrum mountain (8,068), the Indirakoli pass (names of the Chinese maps only) and the top of the Teram Kangri peak, and reaches its south-eastern extremity at the Karakoram Pass. Then alignment of the entire boundary line as described in section one of this article, has been drawn on the one million scale map of the Pakistan side in English which are signed and attached to the present agreement. In view of the fact that the maps of the two sides are not fully identical in their representation of topographical features the two parties have agreed that the actual features on the ground shall prevail, so far as the location and alignment of the boundary described in section one is concerned, and that they will be

determined as far as possible by bgint survey on the ground.

Article 3: The two parties have agreed that:

(i) Wherever the boundary follows a river, the middle line of the river bed shall be the boundary line; and that

(ii) Wherever the boundary passes through a deban (pass) the water-parting line thereof shall be the boundary line.

Article 4: One the two parties have agreed to set up, as soon as possible, a joint boundary demarcation commission. Each side will appoint a chairman (Chaudry Mohammad Aslam for the Pakistani side), one or more members and a certain number of advisers and technical staff. The joint boundary demarcation commission is charged with the responsibility in accordance with the provisions of the present agreement, to hold concrete discussions on and carry out the following tasks jointly.

1. To conduct necessary surveys of the boundary area on the ground, as stated in Article 2 of the present agreement so as to set up boundary markers at places considered to be appropriate by the two parties and to delineate the boundary line of the jointly prepared accurate maps.

    To draft a protocol setting forth in detail the alignment of the entire boundary line and the location of all the boundary markers and prepare and get printed detailed maps, to be attached to the protocol, with the boundary line and the location of the boundary markers shown on them.

2. The aforesaid protocol, upon being signed by representatives of the governments of the two

countries, shall become an annex to the present agreement, and the detailed maps shall replace the maps attached to the present agreement.

3. Upon the conclusion of the above-mentioned protocol, the tasks of the joint boundary demarcation commission shall be terminated.

Article 5: The two parties have agreed that any dispute concerning the boundary which may arise after the delimitation of boundary line actually existing between the two countries shall be settled peacefully by the two parties through friendly consultations.

Article 6: The two parties have agreed that after the settlement of the Kashmir dispute between Pakistan and India, the sovereign authority concerned will reopen negotiations with the Government of the People's Republic of China on the boundary as described in Article. Two of the present agreement, so as to sign a formal boundary treaty to replace the present agreement, provided that in the event of the sovereign authority being Pakistan, the provisions of the present agreement and of the aforesaid protocol shall be maintained in the formal boundary treaty to be signed between the People's Republic of China and the Islamic Republic of Pakistan.

Article 7: The present agreement shall come into force on the data of its signature.

Done in duplicate in Peking on the second day of March 1963, in the Chinese and English languages, both side being equally authentic.

Appendix D

Peace Treaty Between Ladakh and Tibet at Tingmosgang (1684) [372]

The Drukpa (red sect) Omniscient Lama, named My-pham-wang-po, who in his former incarnations had always been the patron Lama of the kings of Ladak, from generation to generation, was sent from Lhasa to Tashis-gang, to arrange the conditions of a treaty of peace-for the Ladak king could never refuse to abide by the decision of the Omniscient One. It was agreed as follows:

1. The boundaries fixed, in the beginning, when king Skyed-Ida-ngeema-gon gave a kingdom to each of his three sons, shall still be maintained.
2. Only Ladakis shall be permitted to enter into Ngarees-khor-sum wool trade.
3. No person from Ladak, except the royal trader of the Ladak Court, shall be permitted to enter Rudok.
4. A royal trader shall be sent by the Deywa Zhung (i.e. the Grand Lama of Lhasa), from Lhasa to Ladak, once a year, with 200 horse-loads of tea.
5. A "Lo-chhak" shall be sent every third year from Leh to

Lhasa with presents. As regards the quality and value of presents brought for all ordinary Lamas, the matter is of no consequence, but to the Labrang Chhakdzot shall be given the following articles, viz:
   (a) Gold dust - the weight of 1 zho 10 times.
   (b) Saffron - the weight of 1 srang (or thoorsrang) 10 times.
   (c) Yarkhand cotton cloths - 6 pieces. (d) Thin cotton cloth - 1 piece.

The members of the Lapchak Mission shall be provided with provisions, free of cost, during their stay at Lhasa, and for the journey they shall be similarly provided with 200 baggage animals, 25 riding ponies, and 10 servants. For the uninhabited portion of the journey, tents will be supplied for the use of the Mission.

6. The country of Ngaress-khor-sum shall be given to the Omniscient Drukpa Lama, Mee-pham-wang-po, and in lieu thereof the Deywa Zhung wil give to the Ladak king three other districts (in Great Tibet).

7. The revenue of the Ngarees-khor-sum shall be set aside for the purpose of defraying the cost of sacrificial lamps, and of religious ceremonies to be performed at Lhasa.

8. But the king of Ladak reserves to himself the village (or district?) of Monthser (i.e. Minsar) in Ngarees-khor-sum, that he may be independent there; and he sets aside its revenue for the purpose of meeting the expense involved in keeping up the sacrificial lights at Kang-ree (i.e. Kailas), and the Holy Lakes of Manasarwar and Rakas Tal.

With reference to the first clause of the treaty, it may be explained that, roughly speaking, king Skyed-Ida-ngeema-gon gave the following territories to his sons:
   a. To the eldest son - The countries now know as Ladak and Purig extending from Hanley on the east to the

Zojila Pass on the west, and including Rudok and the Gogpo gold district.

b. To the second son - Goo gey, Poorang and certain other small districts.

c. To the third son - Zangskar, Spiti, and certain other small districts.

NOTES

1. *Source:* The Indian Society of International Law, The Sino-Indian Boundary (New Delhi, 1962), pp. 12. Reprinted by permission.

   Reproduced from M. C. van Walt van Praag's Status of Tibet: History, Rights and Prospects in International Law. With permission of the author.

Appendix E

Treaty of Chushul

**TREATIES AND CONVENTIONS RELATING TO TIBET
LADAKHI LETTER OF AGREEMENT (1842) [374]**

Translations of the Original Letters Written in Tibetan
Shri Khalsaji Apsarani Shri Maharajah; Lhasa representative Kalon Surkhang; investigator Dapon Peshi, commander of forces; Balana, the representative of Gulam Kahandin; and the interpreter Amir Hah, have written this letter after sitting together. We have agreed that we have no ill-feelings because of the past war. The two kings will henceforth remain friends forever. The relationship between Maharajah Gulab Singh of Kashmir and the Lama Guru of Lhasa (Dalai Lama) is now established. The Maharajah Sahib, with God (Kunchok) as his witness, promises to recognise ancient boundaries, which should be looked after by each side without resorting to warfare. When the descendants of the early kings, who fled from Ladakh to Tibet, now return they will not be stopped by Shri Maharajah. Trade between Ladakh and Tibet will continue as usual. Tibetan government traders coming into Ladakh will receive free transport and accommodations as before, and the

TREATY OF CHUSHUL

Ladakhi envoy will, in turn, receive the same facilities in Lhasa. The Ladakhis take an oath before God (Kunchok) that they will not intrigue or create new troubles in Tibetan territory. We have agreed, with God as witness, that Shri Maharajah Sahib and the Lama Guru of Lhasa will live together as members of the same household. We have written the above on the second of Assura, Sambhat 1899 (17 September 1842).

Sealed by the Wazir,
Dewan, Balana, and Amir Shah.

*

Tibetan Letter of Agreement, 1842

This agreement is made in the interests of the friendship between the Lhasa authorities and Shri Maharajah Sahib and Maharajah Gulab Singh. On the thirteenth day of the eighth month of the Water-Tiger year (September 17, 1842), the Lhasa representative Kalon Surkang, investigator Dapon Peshi, Shri Raja Sahib, sat together amicably with Kunchok (God) as witness. This document has been drawn up to ensure the lasting friendship of the Tibetans and the Ladakhis. We have agreed not to harm each other in any way, and to look after the interests of our own territories. We agree to continue trading in tea and cloth on the same terms as in the past, and will not harm Ladakhi traders coming into Tibet. If any of our subjects stray into your country, they should not be protected. We will forget past differences between the Lhasa authority and Shri Maharajah. The agreement arrived at today will remain firmly established forever. Kunchok (God), Mount Kailash, Lake Manasarowar, and Khochag Jowo have been called as witnesses to this treaty.

Sealed by Kalon Surkhang and Dapon Peshi

NOTES

1. *Source:* W.D. Shakabpa, Tibet: A Political History (New Haven, 1967), pp. 327328.

Reproduced from M. C. van Walt van Praag's Status of Tibet: History, Rights and Prospects in International Law. With permission of the author

*